THE SCHOOL THAT'S INSIDE YOU

THE
SCHOOL
THAT'S INSIDE YOU

PAT MONTGOMERY

Clonlara Press
Ann Arbor, Michigan

Copyright © 2017 by Patricia Montgomery

All rights reserved. No part of this publication may be reproduced, distributed, or transmitted in any form or by any means, including photocopying, recording, digital scanning, or other electronic or mechanical methods, without the prior written permission of the publisher, except in the case of brief quotations embodied in critical reviews and certain other noncommercial uses permitted by copyright law.

For permission requests,
please address:

Clonlara Press
1289 Jewett
Ann Arbor MI 48104

Published 2017 by Clonlara Press
Printed in the United States of America

19 18 17 1 2 3 4

ISBN 978-0-9992933-0-0 (paperback)
ISBN 978-0-9992933-1-7 (ebook)
Library of Congress Control Number: 2017953209

*Dedicated to Chandra and Chai
and to the memory of Jim Montgomery.*

CONTENTS

Foreword ix

Acknowledgments xiii

Introduction xv

1 A Free School Founder in the Making 1

2 The Rest of the Story 21

3 Clonlara: on the Cusp of the Free School Wave 33

4 Moving Beyond Campus 57

5 Extending into Homes 69

6 CLONLARA v. MICHIGAN Department of Education 87

7 CSHBEP'S Overseas Ventures 99

8 Roots of Change and Support Structures 107

9 The Beat Goes On 127

10 Statements From Past Students and Parents 139

FOREWORD

Pat Montgomery, as many a student, school official, politician, and lawyer learned, is a person to be reckoned with, though her origins don't clearly suggest she would be. Born to a first-generation, Irish, immigrant family with eight children, Pat was seventh. She studied to be a Catholic nun from the age of 13 and remained in the order until she was 24. As Pat writes upon leaving the order, "I had been well schooled: use your God-given brain and think for yourself; get your own house in order so that you can effectively serve others; pray for Divine guidance. All of these supported my decision to return to 'the world.'"

Pat uses her brain and service to others in many unique and positive ways throughout her life. Pat's stories of how she navigated the closed society of the convent and the open society of secular life are full of insight, but it is her journey into parenthood that changes her the most. Watching and helping her children learn made Pat decide that conventional school would be detrimental to her children, and so, in 1967, she started her own alternative school, the Clonlara school.

Pat went right to the source to learn how to run an alternative school—she traveled to England to speak with A. S. Neill, the founder of Summerhill School. As they talked about creating a school he told Pat: "Don't start a Summerhill; there's already one of those. Start the school that is inside you."

It turns out, there is a pretty big school inside Pat Montgomery! What started as a small, cozy place for her children to learn with others became a distance-learning school for homeschoolers who enroll from around the world, a model and support for alternative schools in Japan, and an advocate for homeschooling families in courts and legislatures in the United States, as well as in Sweden, Germany, Ireland, the U.K., and elsewhere. Though not a lawyer, Pat's self-directed education in the legal issues that surround alternative schooling are legendary and she is living proof that we can and do learn all the time.

Pat's energy and personal follow-through on these issues helped form and sustain the National Coalition of Alternative Community Schools for well over two decades. She also created or nurtured numerous educational programs at Clonlara, and participated in various efforts to create national and international advocacy groups for self-directed education and community schooling.

Pat and I met through our mutual friend, the late author/teacher John Holt. John's most popular book, *How Children Learn*, was published in 1967, so 2017 marks the 50th anniversary of both John's book and Pat's school. Pat's vision for Clonlara meshed with John's descriptions of active learners. As John writes in *How Children Learn*:

"When we better understand the ways, conditions,

and spirit in which children do their best learning, and are able to make school into a place where they can use and improve the style of thinking and learning natural to them, we may be able to prevent much of this failure. School may then become a place in which all children grow, not just in size, not even in knowledge, but in curiosity, courage, confidence, independence, resourcefulness, resilience, patience, competence, and understanding."

Pat did not want her school to be a competition for grades and status and she took to heart the words of Holt, as well as from many other teachers and theorists who she writes about in her book. Pat's broad understanding of education and how children learn let her shake off the conventional classroom as the best place for learning to occur. Her vision enabled Clonlara to ride the currents of change into the 21st century, such as homeschooling, community service, and the internet.

You will be surprised and cheered by the many twists and turns of Pat's mind and experiences and amazed at how much one person can accomplish with a good team, which Pat always recognizes. Pat Montgomery followed Neill's advice well, and the school inside her is now solidly outside her and in the hands of a new generation.

—*Patrick Farenga*, president and publisher, JohnHoltGWS.com, and founding member of the Alliance for Self-Directed Education (self-directed.org).

ACKNOWLEDGMENTS

Thanks to my family who encouraged me to write this book: Chandra Montgomery Nicol, Ewen Nicol, Chai Montgomery, Amy Hendriksma, and Maddy Hendriksma, and Melanie McKinney.

Thanks to friends who urged me a tad forcefully but without ever crossing the line to nagging: Lori Henderson, Billie Fahrner, Joyce Burkhardt, Carol Gillis, and Shari Maser.

Special thanks to Trish Brewer, a colleague of over twenty-five years, and a seasoned administrator with organizational skills that won't quit. She set up a timeline with me for the duration of this project and exacted weekly progress reports—the things required of people like me who attend to those things on their plates at any one given time. Trish knows how to keep the laser beam steady.

Special thanks, too, to Anne Berggren, a skilled editor, who has been a pleasure to work with.

INTRODUCTION

I have talked about writing a book for nigh on to thirty years. Work got in the way. It ambled about in my brain, this account of my personal experiences as founder and director of Clonlara and its Home Based Education Program. Now, with the benefit of hindsight, I see the past 50 years through the lens of history—the history of two movements: the free school movement and the home school movement. Clonlara, one of hundreds of small, independent schools which blossomed on the educational scene in the Sixties, rode the cusp of the wave of both.

In 2005, when I left the helm of Clonlara, I commented to my daughter, Chandra, who assumed the post of Executive Director, how difficult I found it to write a story that wasn't finished yet. Clonlara's story is still unfolding; it hasn't ended, I said. "It has for you, Mom," she replied. That pronouncement, coupled with the urging I had been getting from others, prompted this effort to tell the tale.

Before proceeding, I must point out some elusive aspects of the very word "school" itself. That word, when used to describe Clonlara, means a place where learners have an equal say in what goes on in their lives. Throughout this book, I use the words free school because that is how the fledgling schools were known when Clonlara was started. As years passed, they have been described as alternative schools, child-led learning centers, student-centered schools, self-designed learning, holistic education, democratic schools … the list goes on.

People—parents, staff, grandparents, marketers, journalists, and others—want a one-word-tells-all descriptor for easy recognition. A Clonlara staff member from the early Seventies, Steve Sandler, phoned me a decade or so later. Steve had been a student at the University of Michigan when we co-taught. Upon graduating with his Bachelor's degree, he moved to Philadelphia to begin medical school. Today, he is Dr. Steven B. Sandler, MD, Child Psychiatrist. When Steve and his wife had children, they joined with a group of people who planned to start a school near Albany, New York, their home. During our telephone conversation, Steve posed the 64-million-dollar question, "What do you call what we did at Clonlara, Pat?" There is no one word. There are many descriptors, but not one that synthesizes what we and the other fledgling schools did then and do now. So, the above listing of words is what we have to work with, and I use them interchangeably herein.

In addition, the word "school" is often used as a coverall that paints ALL institutional schools with the same broad brush. There is no one public school system; not all schools are guilty of being harmful to children and other living things. This fact poses a conundrum: In study after study, researchers find that, among those who call for school reform, very few point a finger at the schools their own children attend. It is all of those other institutional schools that need to change. This underscores yet again the need to clearly define the term.

For me, the key is paying attention to the child, the person who is most affected by what is going on in his/her life. Listen to the words. Observe the body language. Stomach aches, not wanting to go to school more often than once or twice, concerns about what is happening to a classmate—all of these are indicators. They need to be taken seriously, and, if necessary, acted upon for the child's welfare. By their behaviors, and/or their words, they demonstrate whether the fit is right for them. Parents and students are the consumers in the educational marketplace (to use bald terminology). If ever the phrase "the customer is always right" has meaning, it is when the mental, physical, and spiritual health of a child is at stake. Listen. Trust your instincts. Trust your child. That is, perhaps, the most important message a reader may extract from this book.

Throughout my career of 52 years of teaching and administering in public, parochial and alternative schools I have heard parents, especially fathers, respond unsympathetically to reports from a child who is facing bullying or other forms of oppression in school or on the playground.

Get used to it, boy. Life is tough. Just fight back. You'll get over it; I went through it and I turned out alright.

Tell me, Dad, if you were a running coach, would you, say, have your new sprinter start out on the advanced hurdle track? Would you then give him failing marks for not succeeding on his first laps? Almost everyone agrees that, in order to groom a champion in any field, one must treat a beginner with kid gloves, even pampering to some degree. That's the way we treat plants, starting the seedling out in a nursery and watching it gain strength because of the nurturing and care we are giving. Such vigilance makes good sense for potential future champions of any stripe, especially human beings.

Although John Holt saw home schooling as a more efficient, less costly way to help children learn, and gravitated toward keeping them home from schools, he lamented the fact that operating small, innovative schools is a costly affair. The amount of energy and effort required from parents, staff and students in such schools can prove daunting and, sometimes, hazardous to the continuance of the institution. "The life of a free school is, on average, eighteen months," Holt said. Often, disagreement amongst co-founders will cause a school to close, but more often it is lack of operating funds.

As part of earning a Ph.D. from Wayne State University in 1981, I researched North American free schools, using the New Schools Exchange Directory listings. Over 150 of the mailings I sent out came back marked "undeliverable" due to school closures. Three hundred forty-two schools responded.

Of those schools that started around the same time as Clonlara did, and counting only those that comprised both elementary and secondary school levels (serving students from five to eighteen years of age), none remain open today except Clonlara. The reasons for their closings are manifold. Some saw the opportunity to change over into government schools with the advent of charter schools in numerous states; they left their independent, nonprofit status behind. Others faced the cruel realities of financing and chose to close.

Happily, new schools have been opening yearly in the U.S. and all around the world. People are still creating places where children can learn without coercion. They use the resources available in this world that is undergoing technological advances unthought of heretofore. Scientists know more about the development of the human brain now than in past eras, and their findings are fueling necessary changes in the way that we view child rearing and learning.

By telling the story of Clonlara, I hope to demystify some of the long-held fallacies surrounding schools. There are many, and they have probably existed since the 1850s when compulsory schooling laws were put into place. I address some of them in the following chapters. One bears mention here, namely, that schools prepare children for the future.

Consider my father, for example. He was born in 1891, in the decade preceding the turn of a century. His Irish school teachers—from 1897 to 1902 may have believed that they were preparing him for his future. The radio had not yet been invented, and even though Leonardo da Vinci sketched models of motor vehicles and flying machines in the Fifteenth Century, the first mass-produced car, the Model T Ford, was not introduced until 1908 (in the United States at that), and the first jet engine airplane arrived only in the 1930s.

The first television Dad ever saw displayed in a store window appeared when he was 58 years old. He never touched a computer and he probably never even was close to one before his death in 1974, nor did he ever use a cordless telephone, let alone a cell phone. You get the idea. Now, I ask you, could the school he attended three miles from his home in the west of Ireland prepare him for his future? Can any school?

I harbor several hopes for this book. One is that parents, teachers, and youngsters will feel empowered to reclaim responsibility for their own learning, for all aspects of their lives, actually. Another is that anyone drawn to starting a school or a home school will realize that it is very possible. They can even divine, through my example, what not to do. Finally, I hope that those in positions of power over our children—administrators, counselors, policy-makers, politicians and others—are guided to view what they do as a sacred trust.

I attended a talk given by Margaret Mead in Newark, New Jersey in 1963. Part of her address focused on the changes that loomed on the horizon due to advances in technology. This was two years *before* the desktop computer was introduced at the New York World's Fair. Mead said,

"I believe that we adults would be wise to take the hands of our young children and walk together with them into the future, hoping that we don't get left behind".

1
A FREE SCHOOL FOUNDER IN THE MAKING

In 1940, in Greentree Borough just west of Pittsburgh, Pennsylvania, I began first grade at St. Margaret's School, a small four-room schoolhouse with two grades in each room. After my second day, I announced to anyone who would listen that I was going to be a nun like Sister Mary Herman, my teacher. No one ever doubted it—least of all me. So, I dutifully exited eighth grade and, at age thirteen, entered The Villa, the Sisters of Divine Providence preparatory school in Allison Park, Pennsylvania. Two years later I was a member of the Novitiate and on the road to becoming a professed nun. I made no conscious further decision about this, my life choice.

I was the seventh of eight children. My parents were both Irish immigrants who came to America in their separate ways. Mom was scheduled to sail from Cobh (near Cork) on the Titanic. It left ahead of time, so she was booked on the next ship instead and arrived at Ellis Island a year or two before my dad—he from County Clare, she from County Galway.

My uncle, Mike Clancy, a Pittsburgh policeman, was fond of telling us that there were two kinds of Irish: lace curtain Irish and shanty Irish. I thought then that the lace curtain part referred to the neatness of the house; that made my father lace curtain and my mother shanty. As time passed, I learned that lace curtain meant that the owners could afford to put up curtains in the first place, so that made both my parents shanty Irish. Both came from farm families. My father was one of thirteen children, all but one of whom left Ireland around the turn of the century since only one could inherit the farm. The rest were just mouths to feed. There was no work to be had.

Imagine my father's dilemma when he walked the streets of his newfound country (in 1910-13) only to be met by signs posted beneath the "Help Wanted" posters: No Irish Need Apply. (Courtesy of previous immigrants, the White Anglo-Saxon Protestants). But Uncle Sam solved the problem. A recruiting officer for the U.S. Infantry served Dad with citizenship papers in one hand and a draft notice in the other. He was posted to France to fight in WWI.

At the end of the war, soldiers who had emigrated from European countries were given a free trip to their home country before being shipped back to the states. My father declined the gift. "We're Americans now," was how he explained it to my mother who was peeved that he hadn't visited his family near Limerick, County Clare.

Then came the Great Depression. Dad got work wherever he could. The food on our table was from the fruit trees and bushes just outside the door, from the garden, planted each spring and tended by every hand—adult's or child's —that could hoe a row. It was supplemented by the cheese doled out by the U.S. government during these dire years. Rather than take the handout for free, my father worked as a volunteer gardener, planting and minding the nuns' convent at St. Margaret's Parish, and he did general handyman work at the school, church, and convent when he wasn't pounding the pavement for a job or working the land on our acre. His work bartered tuition payments for each of us eight children.

He found a permanent job on the Pittsburgh and Lake Erie Railroad Line (P&LE) in 1933, beginning as brakeman with a schedule of eight hours on, eight hours off, and then on call for his next assignment. When he wasn't sleeping or working the land, he was studying the pages of oversized binders, in self-training to become an engineer—which he successfully did. That was the position from which he retired in 1958.

Like many others who witnessed Black Monday, my father never again put his money in a bank. After I left the convent I took it upon myself one day to clean out his car. The glove compartment was stuffed with uncashed checks from the P&LE; some had been there for years. I said, "Dad, it states right on the face of the check that they don't have to cash these after forty-five days." "They'll cash them when I say they'll cash them," he said. Bookkeepers must have been blue in the face having to carry over his uncashed checks month after month, year after year.

He and my mother, with their burgeoning family, purchased the house I was born into in 1934, just before

I was born. The house was 100 years old with no running water, no indoor plumbing, and no central heating. But it sat on an acre of arable land and they owned it, which was a source of pride to them. This, despite the years of hostilities they were forced to endure from a neighbor who had bid to buy the place but was turned down. A staunch Protestant, she harbored scant regard for the "Papists" next door.

I never knew my parents to take a vacation, per se. Their time in history placed them squarely in survival mode. The picture I carry in mind portrays each of them at work. Mom: digging, planting, weeding, doing the laundry in a Maytag with a hand operated wringer, caring for animals—ducks, geese, turkeys, chickens—tending to the family's basic needs. Dad's daily routine was donning his Oshkosh overalls, pulling out of the driveway for Grand Concourse Station on the South Side, coming home covered with soot and grime, and then poring over his tomes of regulations and procedures of the Brotherhood of Locomotive Engineers, studying to be ready for the numerous tests he had to pass in order to progress in the workforce. My mother took us on the train to visit her sisters in Cleveland every other year or so, thanks to the reduction in fare for railroad employees, but we never all went together anywhere as a family.

It was from my mother that I learned a little about our Irish heritage. I emptied the coffee grounds under the bushes across from the path to the well except on the few times she told me not to do that "because the Little People are there tonight." My sisters explained that she was talking about the fairies and/or leprechauns, and she was dead serious. Voicing disbelief and casting aspersions about her sanity didn't sway her. SHE knew they were there and we better well not disturb them. We didn't... ever.

She told me that the English caused the potatoes to rot in the ground, causing the Great Hunger that plagued the Irish while they watched ships pull out of the docks bound for England, full of seafood caught in Irish waters. At the questioning age of ten, I contested this story once. How could the English (John Bull, as they were known) cause the potatoes to rot in the ground? History books I read years later cited the fact that the tenant farmers were *only* permitted to sow potatoes rather than rotate crops; this cleared the doubt Mom's account had engendered in my ten-year old mind. It took growing older, reading history, and visiting Ireland frequently to appreciate deeply the seeds of cultural awareness that her words and off-the-cuff remarks planted.

From my mother, I learned that surnames told the country of family origin. Who is your new friend? she'd ask when I related my latest after-school escapades. Sally, I replied. I don't know her last name. Well, find out her last name, she ordered. When I told her Sally's last name was Bradfield, she forbid me to play with her again because that was an English surname, though I doubt that Sally or her parents even knew or cared where their ancestors came from. Seven hundred plus years of English oppression of the Irish hung as a millstone around Mom's neck.

Neither of my parents had gone to school beyond sixth grade—sixth "level" was how they referred to it. One would never have known it by listening to my mother talk; her vocabulary was extensive and impressive. She kept abreast of current events and she had an insatiable curiosity and a love of reading that we took for granted.

Of course, sixth level then bore no resemblance to sixth "grade" now; it was probably more akin to community college level nowadays.

As I said, in 1948, at thirteen years of age, I packed my bags and headed for the Villa, the Sisters of Divine Providence convent preparatory school north of Pittsburgh, directly across the road from Providence Heights, the Motherhouse of the Sisters of Divine Providence. From September to June for the next two years, I came home only on weekends, spending much of that time doing my laundry for the coming week. Two years later, I entered the Motherhouse as a postulant, not to return home for the next seven years, and then only for a two-day visit.

There were three steps to profession: postulant (1 year), novice (2 years), and junior professed nun (4 years). The first three of those years, the years of the novitiate, I lived in the spacious Motherhouse, which was designed by a German immigrant who was steeped in the architecture of the castles on the Rhine. It is a showpiece, a beautiful fortress of a place with a spire housing a bell tower rising from its center. In 1950, three hundred nuns called it home—five hundred in the summer months. It sat on seventy-five acres of property, much of it under cultivation and given over to several varieties of apple orchards. It was self-supporting. Animals, raised for meat and milk, grazed alongside the fields of vegetables. There was no shortage of hands to help with the chores. There were over sixty women in the novitiate alone, ranging in age from fifteen to thirty-five. The heavy work—machine work—was done by Jim Shaw, an expert farmer/handyman/manager and a relative of several of the nuns. His family lived in the only single-family house on the property.

The Congregation of the Sisters of Divine Providence (CDP) is a religious Order of women founded by Bishop Wilhelm Emmanuel von Ketteler of Mainz, Germany in 1871, with the help of Marie de la Roche, a Lutheran convert to Catholicism. The nuns fled Kaiser Wilhelm's Germany during the first World War and Hitler's Germany a few decades later to serve in parishes in Ohio and Pennsylvania. Most of the older nuns were born and raised in Europe; some of them spoke only German, a language that all American postulants and novices were taught pro forma.

Here, I entered a training period to embrace the vows of poverty, chastity, and obedience. And here, paradoxically, I enjoyed more "riches" than I had ever had. Running water: hot and cold. A bed of my own. An academic education that I wouldn't otherwise have secured. Serenity, silence, and privacy. Here, this child of Irish immigrants, transported to a strictly German environment, learned about cultural differences, writ large. There was a rigidity typical to German people that contrasted markedly to a more laissez faire attitude of the Irish.

Preparing to embrace the rule of obedience meant adherence to the words of superiors. It meant paying attention to the clock: getting out of bed at the sound of the bell, gathering in the chapel for prayer, filing into the refectory for meals, observing the times to speak and times to be silent. Life was prescribed. The halls of the Motherhouse did not ring with our teenage voices; the rule forbade talking in the hallways; it forbade talking in general. Our time was to be spent dwelling in the Presence of God.

The rule of silence was a Big Item. Other than the necessary speech that had to occur in a work situation, we could speak only at certain designated times. The first time of each day when it was permissible to converse with another person was at the lunch table. Mother Superior rang a small hand bell after a novice had finished reading a passage from the Book of the Saints or some other religious tome. For the next thirty minutes or so we could speak with those sitting around us at the same table. All places at the table were assigned and a hierarchy prevailed here just as it did in chapel seating and in all other places where community members gathered. One's rank depended upon the date one entered the Order and the level of authority one held. This became one's convent "age," replacing the chronological age we'd become accustomed to in the outside world.

The things we could and did talk about were many: plans for feast day celebrations, academic work, the events of our days, comparing notes on musical performances, rehearsing plays that we periodically performed, telling jokes, preparing for student teaching assignments, teaching one another an art or a craft, etc.

Another bell signaled that the time for conversation with neighbors was over. It was not until after dinner on selected nights that this same ritual was repeated. On some nights of the week, the assigned reader read throughout the course of the meal and there was no time for chatting. Following evening chores, we gathered in the conference room for "recreation time." We darned stockings or patched worn areas in skirts, capes, and veils, planned holiday celebration rituals, etc. Not only were we permitted to speak to one another, but we could even leave our seats to touch base with someone who was sitting elsewhere in the room. Once recreation time ended… no more talking. The day ended with night prayer (around 9:00 p.m.) and then began the period known as Grand Silence. It lasted until breakfast on the following day. No talking was allowed during Grand Silence unless lives depended upon it.

Another Big Item was decorum. Now that seems to follow logically when there is a group of teens and young women with energy to burn. Propriety required that we, for example, eat only at the proper times and in the proper place (meal times in the refectory and/or in the evening conference room when the superior passed sweet treats around). It meant that we walk purposefully without swinging our arms, hands at our sides or tucked into the ample sleeves of our habits, heads looking straight ahead.

What a life saver this proved to be for me many years later, on a steaming hot summer's day in downtown Manhattan. I took off my shoes to walk barefoot but the cement was hot enough to fry the proverbial egg. I was sweating profusely. I ached to go to the women's room but there were only sidewalks, noisy traffic, and swarms of people as miserable as I was with no familiar spot to stop and rest. Until, that is, I noticed that people were spewing out of a large office building looking cool and refreshed. I entered only to discover that each person produced an identification badge to the desk sergeant. Rather than turn and exit into the swelter, I struck my most purposeful stride deliberately looking past the sergeant's gaze to a far hallway. It worked. I found a spacious restroom with marble floors and couches well suited to cooling my tootsies.

In the convent milieu, the biggest sin was "worldliness." Talking about home, brothers and sisters, parents, clothes one wore, places one went, things one did before entering the convent was "worldly" and had no place in the behavior of a nun. We were new and inexperienced in this convent setting, so that didn't leave a lot to talk about, at first. It made the rule of silence more reasonable, welcome even. We saw our parents and siblings when they came to visit on designated days, about four times a year except during the Canonical Year of junior novitiate when there was no visiting permitted at all. We wrote letters home once each month. These were screened by the superior, of course, as was any incoming mail.

Cleanliness is next to godliness. This maxim was a mantra for superiors and older nuns, generously passed down to the minions. It was a release valve for our youthful energies, too, since we were assigned to sweep and mop the terrazzo floors, dust all surfaces with oiled rags, clean tubs and commodes, scour kitchen sinks and appliances and leave no stone unturned, as it were. This, three times each day—after every meal. Several times each year we climbed onto scaffolding to wash walls and ceilings and knelt on our knees to thoroughly scrub corners and wax long hallways and the chapel floors.

During a spring cleaning in Sacred Heart Convent in Tarentum, Pennsylvania another young nun and I, accompanied by an older nun, Sister Thecla, were cleaning the hardly-ever-dirty common rooms. We two young ones—tired at the end of a long day sweeping, mopping, washing walls and cleaning wallpaper—were getting giddy and began whispering and chuckling. We were breaking the rule; we realized that Sister Thecla was witness to our misdeeds. She betook herself to a loft area, no doubt to get away from us hooligans. Suddenly, a voice from above, "Sisters, do you have any Dutch Cleanser (a soft scrub powder) down there?" It was Sister Thecla, her German accent unmistakable. "Sure, ve are all Dutch Cleansers down here, Schwester," I replied in my best Cherman imitation as I handed her the container. I knew that we were in for a drubbing when she'd report us to the superior—might as well get some chuckles out of it.

The convent is a different place today than it was before the Nineteen Sixties when Pope John XXIII opened the windows and let fresh air in. I knew it as a serious, somber place full of rules and thou shalt nots. While I was a nun, for example, women religious were not permitted to leave the confines of the Motherhouse or mission house (school parishes to which we were assigned to teach) without having another nun along on the trip. Practically, this meant that if I had to go to the dentist, another nun had to realign her schedule to be with me, like it or not. As a junior professed nun, I took Saturday morning college classes at the Motherhouse and, occasionally at Duquesne University in downtown Pittsburgh. One nun, a music major, had to stay for afternoon classes and, since no nun could travel without a companion, one of the others of us had to stay with her. This often meant not having time to complete teaching lesson plans for the following week or whatever was on the docket for that time, scheduled as it was. Major changes in the mid-Sixties changed that practice and many others.

We were given a poem to memorize in the novitiate that summarizes the value placed on use of time:

> "*I have only just a minute*
> *only sixty seconds in it*
> *forced upon me; can't refuse it*
> *didn't seek it; didn't choose it*
> *but it's up to me to use it.*
> *I must suffer if I lose it*
> *give account if I abuse it.*
> *Just a tiny little minute*
> *but eternity is in it.*"

The words trip off my tongue and fingertips still, and only now, at age 82, am I learning the true meaning of the word "relax."

There was a passage in the Rule of the Order of the Congregation of the Sisters of Divine Providence that some of us junior professed nuns half-jokingly referred to as "the elastic clause." It adjured nuns to report anything they observed about a fellow nun—anything amiss—to the superior for the good of her immortal soul. Well, this encouraged open season on reporting foibles and presumed misbehaviors, world without end amen. I confess that I employed it once myself. I knew very well that the academically smartest novice in my class was forever being called on the carpet by superiors for the sin of intellectual pride. So, when she was assigned to tutor me in chemistry for the lessons I missed while I had my tonsils removed, I took issue with her impatience at my asking questions for clarification. "Don't you even remember THAT formula?" she snippily sighed. In individual counseling with the novice mistress, I allowed at how stupid I felt at not catching on faster, thus making Sr. Patricia go over things until she lost patience. I could only imagine Sr. Pat's next counseling session. I wager that her future efforts to assist another were aided and abetted by the injection of "humility" that the superior undoubtedly supplied. The offshoot of this "elastic clause" engendered in me a distrust of the women around me, a factor that contributed somewhat to my leaving the Order years later.

Humility… that was an interesting concept. The superiors defined humility as "the truth." When a fellow-novice, Sister Paul, was corrected and humiliated publicly for having the stupidity to clean the first aid (sick) room while she waited for the nurse to arrive to take her temperature for suspected fever, I questioned Sister Superior's definition of humility. Why would a sick novice busy herself with chores that were not even assigned to her instead of simply sitting and waiting? The answer was obvious to all of us who knew Sr. Paul. She was a meticulous person, industrious, seldom still when there was work to be done. That was the truth. She was decidedly *not* foolish or unthinking. But the opportunity to train and temper novices seemed to be too great for a superior to pass up, even if it meant bending the definition.

Seriousness was the order of business. I didn't realize it at the time but I was forever juxtaposing, if only mentally, phrases from the book of regulations—making them into puns for my own entertainment and/or seizing harmless chances to enjoy life. A friend, also a former nun, recently reminded me of an event she witnessed once during an annual retreat—a weeklong period of prayer and spiritual renewal when no talking at all was permitted. I walked the outdoor Way of The Cross, stopping at each life-size statue to pray the prescribed prayer for that station. She began minutes afterwards so she was following after me. She noticed that I was praying with my arms outstretched at several of the stations and thought highly of me for adding physical exertion to simple prayers. It was only after seeing this several times that she came to realize that I was actually using the posture to pluck ripe cherries from the trees surrounding the stations. Seeing me plop them in my mouth tempered her opinion of my holiness.

Impressions from my formative years stuck with me, of course, as I aged. They hardened into convictions and rationales. I unconsciously assumed as my own the many, many beliefs I saw in play around me. One in particular stayed with me overlong. On Sunday afternoons in the parish convents, one of the tasks nuns performed was counting all of the money from Holy Mass collections. The rituals surrounding this operation imprinted themselves indelibly on my psyche. We cleared the table, lay down newsprint or butcher paper, rolled up our sleeves and stacked the paper money, then the coins. When it had all been counted and recounted for accuracy and when all the coins had been wrapped, we threw the newsprint/butcher paper into the trash, washed the table well, and finally bathed our hands and arms with Murphy's soap. The coins especially left a black, metallic residue. The term "filthy lucre" aptly applied.

Maybe this ritual was not the reason I couldn't ever learn to fundraise for Clonlara School or seek necessary monies for a development fund, etc., but I suspect it contributed. As did the fact that I was raised during the depression in a family that specialized in hand-me-downs and squeezed every penny. And then again, I had taken a vow of poverty, which meant I seldom had to even touch money. If I needed a new pair of shoes, I simply showed the worn ones to the superior; after a few days, I'd find a new pair on the chair in my sleeping cell.

My life wasn't all brimstone, though; I don't want to give that false impression. I was a content, focused member of a community which was my family. For the three years we were in training at the Motherhouse, we spent many a weekend afternoon or evening roller-skating or playing basketball at Kearns Hall, one of the areas reserved for our use. Summertime found us on the softball field outside when we weren't taking lessons from the head of the Tamburitzans, a Duquesne University music and dance group of some renown. We learned folk dances from other lands, square dances, line dances… the lot. I was one of the tall (5 ft. 7½ in.) gals so I took the male role in folk dances. We performed for the older nuns on special occasions like holidays and holy days.

Music was a vital part of our lives, especially during the novitiate years. We all, with small regard for how well we could carry a tune, sang at every High Mass in the chapel. We spent long hours learning the hymns, practicing with a pianist, polishing, and then finally practicing in the huge chapel with the organ. If they ever have a name-that-tune game show featuring religious hymns in Latin or English, I'd win hands down, and if I got to sing the song on top of that, sheer heaven.

Once or twice a year we'd hike from the Motherhouse

to the closest convent of the Order in Pine Creek (Glenshaw, Pa.), a seven-mile trek one way. The contemplative silence times were balanced with times of high energy output and noisy activity.

Following the first year as a postulant, I became a junior novice and began what was known as "the canonical year." This was to be a year devoted to immersion in the rules of the Order. No contact with outsiders was to occur. No relatives or friends could visit; I could write letters home, but make and receive no phone calls except in cases of a death in the family. No secular studies. Only spiritual readings, Bible study, canon law, lives of the saints and the like.

During the next year, as a senior novice, I did two years' worth of high school studies to be ready to leave the confines of the Motherhouse and enter the world of the teaching nun. For two weeks that year, we donned black veils, went to the assigned mission house, and student-taught under the tutelage of a master teacher. These were the days when the Catholic schools were filled to capacity. It was 1953. I was eighteen years old. Some of the students I dealt with were sixteen years old. Thus began my career as a teacher. It was permissible in those days to teach without a teaching credential and with such minimal preparation as long as a person was taking college classes and working toward a teaching certificate. Duquesne University sent professors to the Motherhouse in Allison Park each Saturday and during the summer months to assure that we were working toward an (eventual) degree and teaching certificate.

Teacher was a catchall name given to the host of jobs

that had to be done in a Catholic parish. Janitor, choir director, drama coach, parent counselor, student counselor—all of these jobs and more were filled by whomever was appointed by the Sister Superior, who wore her share of other hats, too. She was often the Principal of the school, liaison with the Parent-Teacher group, school accountant, and more. During my eight years of teaching as a nun, I was, in addition to my assigned classroom teaching, the janitor, play writer and director, choir director, playground attendant, counselor to students and to parents, and unofficial co-counselor to new staff members. The fact that I had no prior training for any of these posts mattered very little. God will provide was the usual platitude that came with the assignment, and wonder of wonders! that's how it generally panned out.

Once I was told to act as choir director for the 600 student church choir. I love to sing and that was my only qualification. Only the very adept (and initially disgusted) organist was aware that I could not sight-read music, could not play an instrument, and had not been trained as a choir director. Fools rush in! Mine is not to reason why; mine is but to do or die.

During my first year of teaching at St. Norbert's in 1953, I was frequently called to task for befriending the kindergartners on the playground. I even allowed one little tyke to swing the long black rosary hanging from my waistband. This prompted a lecture on authority and discipline. It went like this: in older, wiser times, the children and the teacher were separated by a large riser upon which sat the teacher's desk. It stood in front of the room in a commanding position. A teacher was poised to look down upon the student, holding a proper, authoritarian position that required the reverse—that the student would look up to the teacher. When that podium was removed, the teacher was forced to be on the same level with the student, removing stature from the teacher. When a nun is assigned to playground supervision duty, she must retain a position apart from the children, keeping them at arm's length away from her at all times. No touching, no putting arms around their shoulders, and definitely not having them touch her, especially her blessed rosary. This demeanor will instill respect in a child and the position of authority that a teacher should hold will not be compromised. Lecture over.

For the first time in my life as a religious, I was certain that this assessment and advice was wrong. Even though the five-year-olds were not the ones I was teaching at that time, I instinctively knew that a base of trust could be established between them and an adult simply by my enjoying their company and vice versa. The rosary swinger stopped immediately upon my telling her to, in itself a sign of respect. I then had sense enough to tuck the attractive accessory into my pocket to render it less tempting to her and her pals.

Speaking *to* them instead of *at* them invited the same, normal response from them, I learned. Discipline, it seemed to me, is not instilled from the outside by training and nagging and punishing and rewarding. It comes from the inside, from imitating the good example of thinking, feeling, open, honest people, and from a child's striving to please loving, caring, nurturing people who reciprocate in kind. Though it railed against the grain of being obedient, I utterly rejected Sister's reproach while attempting to discover compassionate ways to analyze and understand human behavior.

I taught in seven parish schools in my eight years of teaching as a Sister of Divine Providence, on every grade level from third through eighth grade. There were anywhere from a low of 45 students in a grade to a high (one year) of 75. Teaching became my passion. No surprise there, since my mission was to serve God in any capacity assigned by my superiors and since this was, basically, a teaching Order of nuns.

Finally, at age 24, it occurred to me that I could live a good life and serve God without wearing a religious habit and without living exclusively in a community of women. I had been well schooled: use your God-given brain and think for yourself; get your own house in order so that you can effectively serve others; pray for Divine guidance. All of these supported my decision to return to "the world."

Mother Superior walked me through the procedure (when she wasn't pleading with me to change my mind and rid it of the devil's wily temptation). I would have to write a letter to the Pope, the highest authority for this Community, to seek permission to be released from vows of poverty, chastity, and obedience. Did the Pope ever say no? I asked. Yes, he could, she warned. It was wait-and-see for about five months until I received the official O.K. from Rome.

Years later, when home schooling parents and I had to meet with a school board here or a superintendent there or a prosecuting attorney or a judge, I'd slough off questions about why I wasn't cowed by these august people of power.

Ha! I had been required to petition the Pope; what could be scarier than that?

I left with a keen appreciation of what those formative years had given me. The calm, the silence, the prayer, the music… gifts I would never lose. A college education, also—an anomaly in my family where I was the only one of eight who was given the chance for education and credentials well beyond the high school level. In fact, most of my siblings did not even graduate from high school. I treasure, above all, two specific lessons that living and growing in the Divine Providence Congregation taught me:

> 1) an unbending reliance upon Divine Providence, and

> 2) abandonment to the Holy Spirit—the spirit that "blows where it wills."

I left, confident that whatever life held for me in a new chapter, wherever my vocation lay next, I was ready, thanks to my experiences in every respect until that point.

2
THE REST OF THE STORY

On May 22, 1962, I signed away my convent name, Sr. Norma Jean, and became once again, Pat Clancy. I left a convent world that was uniform, controlled, and predictable for one which was none of the above. I was then a twenty-five-year-old woman who had skipped all of the trials, tribulations, pleasures and displeasures which are part and parcel of growing to adulthood in this society; I understood precious little about the culture I returned to. I was chronologically twenty-five but emotionally fourteen years old. With me I brought all of the well-entrenched lessons of my Novitiate—trust, obey, defer to age and rank, put your hands in your sleeves and walk with your head bowed, and think for yourself. The last one was an emotional life-saver.

My neck and forehead were stark white, an eerie face frame caused by years of being swathed by a veil and headpiece. Off I went to Horne's Department Store in downtown Pittsburgh; the clerk at the make-up counter saw me coming. By the time she had collected all of the Max Factor pancake make-up, eye shadow, blush, and numerous shades of lipsticks for when I wore blue or red or orange, etc., etc., etc., I had racked up a bill of over $200.00. This exceeded the amount of money I received upon leaving the convent by $100.00. So, I told her I'd purchase only one or two items right then and come back again for the others. She said the she'd be back at that counter on Tuesday. I labored over my dilemma of having to purchase more than I wanted or even needed, but I had given my word and I was bound to it. On Monday I telephoned the store and told the receptionist the whole story, apologizing that I wouldn't be able to keep my end of the deal and would she please explain this to the cosmetics clerk tomorrow. Her response—confusion, a yawn, and a few huhs?—taught me a lesson about truth-telling in this world I now inhabited.

More than one person inquired, or otherwise insinuated, about whether nuns are lesbians. I responded from my own experience: early in the Novitiate we were cautioned about "particular friendships." Give your love to God, not to a human was the message. This coupled well with the "elastic clause" encouraging reporting others' infractions to superiors. I knew no nuns who were lesbians.

One unfortunate offshoot of ignoring human friendship in general had a debilitating effect on me. I simply ignored the need, never wanting to get close to anyone, confide in anyone, share hopes and fears and dreams with anyone, especially with another woman. It took years to even recognize that I had this malady; it took excellent models to teach me how to reverse it. My own two adult children became my role models, as did Billie Fahrner, a co-worker at Clonlara for many years, Sandy Hurst, Director of Upattinas School in Glenmoore, PA, and Lu Vorys, an NCACS luminary from Paonia, CO. Ironically, perhaps, some others who contributed to my much-needed education were the nuns themselves when I re-united with the Order and with individuals in the mid-Eighties.

Back to Duquesne University I trudged in 1960. Even though I had (then) been teaching for seven years, I had no teaching certificate nor had I earned a college degree. That became my first order of business. Armed with a Bachelor's degree and a teaching certificate, I accepted the suggestion that a former nun (who had left the Order a few years before I). She invited me to interview in the public school district where she taught. I accepted a position with Nankin Mills Public Schools not far from Detroit, Michigan.

The transition from teaching in a Catholic school to teaching in a public school brought more surprises than I ever could have imagined. As a teaching nun in a teaching order of women religious, I was expected to devote every available hour to preparing for my role, and I did. Each nun was allotted one trunk to have shipped to whichever mission house the Mother Superior assigned her for the school year. Clothing—two serge habits: one for Sundays; one for workdays—and personal effects took up very little space. The remainder was filled with teaching paraphernalia: classroom decorations collected or handmade, teaching materials gathered, chalk holders, prizes for students, swatches of textured cloth and paper, select paint brushes, and the like.

The time left over from community and personal prayer time, mealtime, and clean-up time was spent preparing lessons, correcting papers, researching new methods, and writing daily lesson plans which were submitted by Sunday afternoon to the principal for approval. Taking work home from school to do in the evening hours was *de rigueur*.

Talking ill of parents, students, or fellow teachers was considered to be the height of unprofessional behavior, not to mention, uncharitable. Problems that arose in relating to any members of this group were to be addressed with the superior who was almost always doubled as school principal. In short, teaching was not a job; it was a life. We walked, talked, prayed, fretted, planned, and performed as teachers every waking hour, and often dreamed of it at night.

Catholic school classrooms were filled to capacity for most of the Fifties and Sixties. It was customary for one teacher to have 50 or more students in the room. Once, during my fourth year of teaching, I started the year with a mere forty (40) students in St. Mary's School in Glenshaw, Pennsylvania third grade. Come November, the lay teacher of the other third grade classroom across the hall from mine left her post with no advance notice;

she decided to enter a convent to become a nun in the Franciscan Order. Her students were assigned to me and my classroom number ballooned to seventy-five (75) for the remainder of that year.

In my public school role, I noticed that most teachers ignored the art and craft of classroom decorating, often leaving bulletin boards, walls, and chalk board bare or using store-brought items for Halloween, Valentine's Day, etc. Only a few, other than the art teacher, bothered to display children's work. Scarcely any teacher took work home to do in the evenings; that was what paid prep time was for.

My biggest shock was hearing many teachers badmouth parents and students, usually in the teachers' lounge, loud enough for anyone to hear—counselors, coaches, student teachers, even the principal. Parents' attitudes, style of dress, the cars they drove—students' stupidity, churlishness, dress, etc., were all fair game.

Classrooms, by state law, could not exceed 33 students (1962- 67). What a piece of cake, thought I. No janitorial work, handling gym classes, directing massive choirs, teaching art or biology classes. I actually received pay for time spent preparing classwork and was only asked to do playground duty (supervision) occasionally.

Teachers viewed new teaching methods and approaches, for the most part, with suspicion and resistance. Most teachers were interested in keeping the lid on classroom behavior and doing the tried and true (even if this proved to be boring or a waste of time to the youngsters). Parents, and some kids too, expected that specific things would be taught, preferably in a manner not too different from what the parents themselves had experienced when they went to school.

The subject matter covered was determined by the textbook which was produced by university professors or committees consisting of university professors and teachers, assigned by state boards of education, and rubber stamped by local school boards. There was not much time for supplementary activities—those enlivening rewards that most kids looked forward to—given the amount of time for each class. Both parents' and students' expectations that a certain amount of material would be covered over a certain amount of time was fairly set. After all, the child's so-called level of readiness for the next grade was at stake. These concepts proved to be held by both Catholic and public school folks alike. I discovered that in this regard, Catholic schools mirrored public schools, minus the habit and the use of Loyola University textbooks.

Schools of Education were still pushing the lecture method of teaching in all grade levels. The teacher was the authority in the classroom, a benevolent dictator at best. The principal's job was to maintain order in the school and s/he relied on each teacher to police (a word customarily used) the class to maintain order and relative quiet.

It was indeed a rare and unusual person who sought to make the process palatable for youngsters and for herself, the teacher. Alene Greene was such a person. She taught sixth grade in a room of Mack School in Ann Arbor that was a distance removed from the rest of the classrooms. My fifth-sixth grade combined classroom was in closest proximity, a favor I learned to appreciate over the span of a year there. It was a place apart in many more ways than one. Language Arts classes, for example, were turned into mock radio broadcasts. Kids auditioned for the parts of announcer, timekeeper, technician, audience members, emcee, guest artists, and critics. It was an exciting, lively thing that engaged all class members. Kids discussed the class as though it were a show they were part of and they poured lots of outside time into making it happen. More often than not, Alene would cap this whole project off with a trip to a local radio station where the gang could put on a real show over real mikes. She planned events like this on her own time, having to finagle to take the field trip and spending arduous hours assuring the principal that the class was indeed covering the material in grammar and literature even though it all just looked like fun and games to the conventional observer.

Alene was exceptional! She requested and received permission to start teaching a class of, say, third graders and stay with that same group until they went on to junior high (grades seven to nine). Needless to say, she did not frequent the teachers' lounge. I felt honored to interact with Miss Greene's group during playground duty, on the stairs, and in the hallway we shared.

School was synonymous with control. The message from the adults to youngsters was sit down, keep quiet, listen, and repeat after me. Rewards and punishments were the carrot and stick that adults used to lure kids into compliance.

Student teachers and first-year teachers were told by veterans, "You're enthusiastic now, but that won't last long." This was followed by a recitation of that "reality" which would seep in to take the shine off their youthful, therefore temporary, eagerness. Dedicated men and women stood out from the crowd which was increasingly peopled by those attempting to avoid the draft by taking an easy route through college: Mickey Mouse education courses.

Both teachers and parents, more often than not expressed hackneyed attitudes toward children. They are blank slates needing to be trained, empty vessels needing to be filled, playdough needing to be shaped. Kids are objects to be manipulated and managed; not human beings to be engaged in the process. It was as though the proper posture of a student should be to keep quiet and listen then regurgitate what he heard the teacher say. Jump through the hoops to get the prize which was, in the main, not to have to be in this prison-like setting any more. For far too many, the boredom of school was replaced, upon graduation, with the boredom of the work world. Life was a series of preparations. Kindergarten prepared a child for grade school; grade school prepared him for high school; high school prepared her for work; and work preceded retirement. Then a person was free to enjoy life and do things one chose to do and would willingly do without being paid for it.

Parents were eager to have their children fit into school. In 1967 in Burns Park public school in Ann Arbor a full fifty percent of the five year olds were under psychiatric care, being medicated, a teacher there told me. They were anxiety-prone; they competed for her undivided attention; always tried to be in first place, reacted badly if they did not earn a star or other reward. They couldn't follow orders, had trouble paying attention, they didn't know how to share and they lacked the skills to function successfully as part of a group.

Both teachers and parents seemed to be afraid of kids, especially of teenagers. They emphasized the importance of maintaining discipline, using that word as a euphemism for punishment. The reverent atmosphere of my Catholic school environment was gone; yet the dictatorial stance of both teachers and administrators still held sway.

Christopher Jenkins, educational historian, appealed to teachers to break the lock-step system. He cautioned that children are compelled to be in the classroom so we, as teachers, ought to make things enjoyable and alive for them, at the very least. I resonated with that concept. And I found a lot of sustenance for an opposing view from other authors and activists as well. Sylvia Ashton Warner's work and books became my mainstay as did Haim Ginott's and Carl Jung's. I took classes at the University of Michigan at night and during summer to complete a Master's degree in child development. The fresh, open ideas of professors like David Angus and many another didn't seem to penetrate down to those engaged with children in classrooms.

It was here that I was introduced to A.S. Neill and his life work, Summerhill. Treat them like the intelligent, feeling, involved people that they are. Trust them and trust yourself as a parent and a teacher. Most of all, lose the stage-front-and center position and share humanity with all.

Along the way, in 1963, Jim Montgomery and I had married. Chandra was born in 1963; Chai in 1964. Jim had been an only child and having two in relatively short order left him in awe and wondering much of the time. He wasn't alone in those sentiments, I must admit. Even when I was leaving the hospital, having given birth to Chandra, I positively marveled as the fact that the nurse carried the baby to the exit door, then turned and placed her in my arms. I was gripped with the realization that she was letting this tiny being go home with us. Just the three of us—Jim, baby and me in the car. What am I supposed to do with her, I wondered? It didn't take long to find out!

It dawned on Jim and me a short time later that we hadn't had a minute to ourselves in a week and a half, so filled were our hours and minutes with the new arrival. That evening, when I placed her, soundly sleeping, in her crib we decided to go for a walk together and blissfully left the house, heading for the park nearby. We had gone less than a block when we looked at one another and said simultaneously, "the baby... she's alone." We bolted back and we both agreed that for at least a few years henceforth, we would be willing slaves.

Jim had been an only child. A year later, with the arrival of Chai, he learned what it's like to have two little ones in the family. He was enamored by their interactions, and sometimes he was conflicted by them. Once when they were toddlers, they were chittering at one another over some disagreement. Jim looked at me as though to say what do we do now? I addressed the two scrabblers and said, "Could you two consider being agreeable to one another?" Chandra, the elder at age four put her hands on her hips and replied, "This is the way brothers and sisters are supposed to act, Mom." Chai nodded his agreement to that. Just how she came upon this advanced knowledge, escaped me, but I couldn't refute it. Nor could Jim. Happily, the dickering subsided with the query.

Step by step, phase by phase, we awakened to the innate intelligence of these two creatures. They had a sense of what was happening around them, even when it was unspoken, as though they could read thoughts and intentions. Body language, too. They were a heady mix of the spiritual and the practical.

I saw with my own eyes their stages of development and I realized that when I was a teacher all those prior years, I had no idea what the journey was for a child to reach the age that I was teaching at that time. They were all 8 year olds or 10 year olds or 16 year olds. That's where life began as far as I was concerned. Little did I know that the lessons each child had learned up until the year I entered the scene were a vital part of who she was. The continuum concept was nowhere on my horizon in those days.

My dissatisfaction with the system of schooling that virtually everyone in the dominant culture took for granted finally took a shape. I was no longer just teaching other people's children; I was responsible for providing for our own two. This riveting thought propelled me to decide that I should start a school for my own two and for anyone else who may join us. It would look nothing like a conventional school. Childhood is too short a span to be squandered.

I went to visit one of my heroes, A.S. Neill in Leiston, England in the spring of 1967. I told him of my plan. He asked whether I had a religion. When I replied Roman Catholic, he threw up his hands and said that I would have a whale of a time maintaining a free school because the priests would come in and order the children about and punish them. I assured him that this would not be a school with any connections to organized religion.

"Don't get me wrong," he said. "I have the greatest respect for Jesus Christ. He practiced what he preached. He didn't own the sandals on his feet." Then after a period of silent pondering, he added, "I'd hate to show Him through the Vatican today."

Then, a little later… "Don't start a Summerhill; there's already one of those. Start the school that's inside you."

3
CLONLARA: ON THE CUSP OF THE FREE SCHOOL WAVE

On October 2, 1967 Clonlara—a preschool/nursery for three and four-year olds—opened its doors with eight students: Chandra, Chai, and six other youngsters whose parents had responded to an invitation, mostly by word of mouth. The plan was to begin with these youngsters, learn as I went along, and add an age each year until children of all elementary school ages were included. I was teacher, administrator, janitor, van driver, admissions director, and Mom (then and for years to come), assisted by a college student. It would be a place where kids could play, make choices, play, follow their interests, live, play, and learn to get along in a group of people interested in doing the same things. A place where youngsters and adults could be themselves. A place where the spotlight would be on the child as s/he lived and learned without interference from even well-meaning adults for the sake of control and molding or making changes for a good fit. A place where mutual respect and support were standard issue.

Learning by doing was a mesmerizing task which, coupled with being with the young ones every day, consumed almost every ounce of my energy with barely enough left for the myriad administrative parts. There were government forms to fill and file, regulations to study and implement, equipment and supplies to order, phones to answer, and so much more.

I petitioned my sister, Kitty Wallace, to move from her home and job in Pittsburgh, PA to assume the post of office manager. Her own children were raised and on their own, and she had made a career of bookkeeping and just the sort of work that Clonlara now required. In 1971, she accepted the role. Not only did she use her excellent administrative skills on Jewett Street, but she became involved in virtually every aspect of the community life of Ann Arbor. She founded and led the Irish-American Association. She worked with the Mayor's office on the Sister-City, international exchange program. She co-chaired the Multi-Ethnic Society's work, especially its annual celebration on Main Street where performers from many different countries performed, and where food and drink from the member organizations was available to a partying public. She was well-known in our city and in the state.

When I was downtown, Kitty was *my* sister, and when we were at Clonlara, I was *her* sister. Kitty announced at one city meeting that she promised "to come here from Pittsburgh for one year in order to get Clonlara's office up and running well. That was 20 years ago. I am either a slow worker or I've lost track of time." That brought laughter from every listener; we all knew she was wrong on both counts.

I was the head of Clonlara. Kitty was its heart. Kitty died in November 1991, due to a sudden resurgence of intestinal problems.

This band of three and four-year olds—eight little ones—and I spent our days being and doing. I started each day with an activity that interested me, and each of them did likewise. Sometimes, we were even all interested in a single given thing, but mostly, there were any number of things that caught each one's attention.

Most of the consumable materials we used were the cast-offs of a society that was far too often wasteful. Every Thursday, for instance, we took a field trip to the University Microfilms outside of town, backed the van into a loading dock and watched while workers stacked the end rolls of seamless computer paper spindles that were too short for another large book run. These were perfect for us to use for drawing, painting, making borders for the walls, drawing the outlines of our bodies on... and many other projects. Bell telephone supplied us with unused cables, each containing multi-colored strands of wiring that found its way into wire sculptures, bracelets, necklaces, replacements for cloth ribbons, tea pot handles—just name it. A printing company in the next town allowed us to empty their recycle bins filled with vellum and cardboard, expensive materials that would have otherwise been out of our reach. All of these materials augmented our art closet stock.

We took advantage of the surrounding community in much the same way, using the school passenger van to investigative and enjoy city parks, libraries, museums, cemeteries, gravel pits, farms, nursing homes—any place where one of us had an interest or a question to ask. Some trips became woven into the fabric of our days for years to come: watching a pair of swans migrate to a nearby lake to mate and bear cygnets, visiting Kellogg's cereal plant in Kalamazoo, arranging with Mr. McCalla to visit his farm every spring to see lambs being born, peeps hatching or piglets being born.

In cemeteries, for example, we discovered bas relief grave markers that allowed us to take crayon and carbon images and find names that sounded German or Irish or Italian, etc. This led to discussions about the founders of Ann Arbor and the multi-ethnic groups several parents belonged to. Once—when the children were considerably older than pre-school age—we found a section that contained a cluster of graves that held the remains of young children, some who had died in their nursery years. The caretaker explained that there had been a flu epidemic that year.

Rather than duplicate on school property the grand playgrounds available in local parks, we just went to the parks on any given day. The same with sports activities. We lacked the funding to lay a track on the grounds so we went to the Par-Course at the Washtenaw County Farms. For swimming, we went to the Ann Arbor Y each week. The community was our extended classroom and we benefitted by living in a well-endowed one. We were a working model of Mr. Roger's neighborhood in a lot of ways!

The notion of referencing original sources grew organically in us. From the earliest days in the pre-school group, for instance, when we heard a siren outside that signaled a fire truck was passing, we took to the van and pursued the matter first-hand. The observations we made fed more than just our curiosity; they prompted discussions and debates that could never have been authentically dealt with through reading or telling about it. At the scene of a dormitory fire, for example, we saw a dead squirrel. The death probably had nothing whatsoever to do with the fire, but it was there, close to where we stood. Matters of life and death and what happens when things die and why; what happens to human beings when they die. These discussions went on for days afterwards.

Different belief systems were explained by a Catholic or Jewish or Muslim child as well as by agnostics and atheists. It was most enlightening for each of us, regardless of what our ages were.

For me, the early days of operation greatly resembled graduate level classes at a university: Starting A Free School 101, and Kids Below the Ages I Had Ever Taught 102. It was hands-on learning writ large!

My assistant and I had the chance to observe each child, make mental and literal notes, share what we learned with one another and with parents and build upon what we observed/learned. One striking lesson for us was how ingrained in conventional, knee-jerk reactions we adults were. It took conscious effort to work past the common beliefs that just because kids are small doesn't mean they don't wonder and worry and reach sensible conclusions. Molly, a three-year-old, shared her concerns about Jane, her teen-aged older sister: Jane should not go over to Bob's house and stay overnight, she said aloud to the group one morning, with severity and warning in her voice. (Bob was a single forty-year-old, divorced neighbor of theirs.) All present solemnly agreed.

Rochelle, the mother of a four-year old, Dan, asked for a *tete-a-tete* after sessions one day. She explained that he had undergone several operations on the bones in his leg, the result of a birth defect. It caused him to limp and to tire easily. Rochelle had taken him to another pre-school but he couldn't stay there because the adults expected him to go beyond his capacity and try one more game or one more running race, though he told them he couldn't. They also urged him to get right into an activity without holding back or being shy. She was delighted that those things didn't happen here, and that we trusted youngsters to know what's best for themselves. Then she confided that Dan had a younger sister, Mary (age three), but that Mary couldn't attend pre-school (though she dearly wanted to be with Dan) because she wasn't even toilet trained yet.

"Could you counsel me; what am I doing wrong?" she asked. I was shocked that, first, she would think that a child so young ought to be toilet trained for the sake of attending a pre-school; and, second, that she was asking me as though I knew what was good for her child. Rochelle and I were about the same age; we both had children, and we both wanted the best for them. But that didn't qualify me as more knowledgeable than she about Mary. I could only agree with her assessment that Mary needed time to develop and to live through the strain that the whole family endured because of her son's needs. I simply assured her that I knew how to change diapers when necessary and that this was not an impediment to Mary's joining our group.

Her investment of wisdom in presumed authority figures struck me as being a major part of the problem of systems in general: education, health, finance, government…

the lot! It allows an individual to hand important matters over to a perceived expert and shut down her own capacity to decide and to act. I saw the same attitudes at play again and again when parents voiced concern about getting a child ready for first grade (in conventional school) or whether a child will be ready for college if he didn't attend conventional school or, years later, how a local public school superintendent would react to a family's decision to home school.

Ruth, mother of Ellen and Richard, worried that Richard would not be welcome at Clonlara because he frequently chose to sit with Mom in their van rather than follow his sister into the building, or he would walk right through the house and out to the playground where he'd enjoy the swings and slide. Richard, at four, wasn't ready to mix and mingle. Ruth needed assurance that this behavior was normal and that when he was ready he'd join the group. To this day, she marvels at his innate wisdom. He did eventually feel comfortable enough to let her leave him. He became an active, albeit shy, member of the class, and in just a few short years he learned to read with no prompting from anyone.

There was a time when we all did join together for a single purpose: the meeting. When there was an announcement to be made or a trip to be planned, we called a meeting. At first, an adult would chair the meeting, but soon youngsters, too, took over that role. It was at these times that we experienced the power of having a fledgling family at one's beck and call. It was at these times that rules were made and accepted with the consent of all ... or rejected. It was at these times that we became an egalitarian society—where we *lived* democracy. It became clear that a simple majority decision left 49 percent of us dissatisfied, as though our opinions and views didn't matter. So, every attempt was made to listen attentively to one another and to negotiate with one another, to include the voice and view of each. We learned the Quaker approach—consensus.

The wisdom of the group was impressive. Sara, age 4, rang the bell that summoned us all several days in a row. As events unfolded, it became clear that she was voicing the same concerns in each successive meeting: Jason is teasing me. She wanted to bring it out in the open so that we'd all be aware of the facts as she saw them. She wanted us all to share her "burden." It was becoming a refrain. The advice and counseling that members of the group offered in these sessions seemed lost on her. Finally, Jason was asked to explain his behavior.

Yes, he admitted. I do tease Sara because she waits for me at the gate every morning and asks me if I am going to tease her that day and because she hides my lunch and my hat. Here was a voice we had only heard in staccato responses before.

This relatively benign matter launched us into an acceptance of some of life's most critical issues: living peaceably in society; relating harmoniously with one another. It also launched—though we weren't fully aware of this at the time—our approach to non-punitive problem solving.

Individuals can look at the same things and see them differently. Disagreement—conflict—is as natural to the scheme of things as breathing in and out is. If we learn to face differences head-on, painful as that may be, we will develop skills for solving problems. Most problems can be solved in this direct, deliberative way.

A prime example of this approach happened when we were scheduled to leave for the Toledo Zoo one morning, a trip happily anticipated by all of the three and four year olds. When I inspected the van, however, I discovered not one but two flat tires. Sadly, I announced that we would have to postpone the trip. Disappointment abounded; some wept aloud.

Maryann, age 3, tearfully sobbed, "Pat, you should not tell us that we cannot go." Not wanting to add injury to insult by reciting the obvious, I responded, "Maryann, what could I say that would change this?"

She caught her breath along with a modicum of composure and said, "You could just tell us that the tires were bad and we could fix them."

Others agreed with her, hoping against hope. "How could we do that?" I asked.

"My uncle has a gas station and he would do it. I could phone him."

I stretched the phone cord to reach where she sat, realizing the futility of her suggestion. She phoned him. He brought the service truck to our driveway and repaired one tire and changed the other while we watched from the window. We left for the zoo just an hour or so later than planned. Simply setting the problem out in the open for all to know and working toward a reasonable, logical solution together had saved our trip. This lesson stayed with me from that instance on.

There is an Irish saying that, paraphrased, sums it up: When there are five Irishmen in a room, there are eight opinions. Then there is the Biblical mandate, Matthew 18:15: "Moreover if your brother shall trespass against you, go and tell him his fault between you and him alone: if he shall hear you, you have gained your brother." And James Baldwin said, "Not everything that is faced can be changed, but nothing can be changed until it is faced." These truisms were our guides in crafting a step-by-step procedure that would assure that we honestly, openly, frankly examined differences and disagreements from each person's point of view and then laid plans to correct them.

1) First, the parties having difficulties had to make this known to one another.

2) Second, if that solved the matter, all well and good, but if it didn't, then they sought out a trusted friend or two who could help them work toward a solution.

3) Finally, if that didn't work, one or both parties brought the issue to the attention of the entire group—using the meeting as the forum—and the collected wisdom of the group most often got the job done.

We were replacing the convention of having rules made by people who are not necessarily even present in the day to day goings-on (school boards, trustees, etc.). We were replacing a call for punishment and retribution (euphemistically called "discipline") with knowledge about how our actions affect others and how intentions are unseen motivators and need to be revealed in words and in actions.

Over the years, this was the method we used to handle disputes as non-threatening as Jason's and Sara's push-me-pull-you game and as serious as a teenage boy's threat of bringing drugs to campus years later. At the annual conferences of the National Coalition of Alternative Community Schools, we learned that the indigenous people of the U.S. and Canada governed in these humane ways, as did the Maori people in New Zealand and communities of Mennonites the world over.

In 1977, we learned that Albert Eglash, a British psychologist, introduced a practice called Restorative Justice, a theory of justice that emphasizes repairing the harm caused by criminal behavior. This is accomplished through cooperative processes that include all stakeholders. It can lead to transformation of people, relationships and communities. It codified for us the practices we had initiated early on, in the youngest to the oldest groups, as an equitable, humane way of setting things right when there were conflicts. It allowed us to focus upon remedying a wrong without resorting to punishing, and it prepared all to be able to handle bigger conflicts as we aged.

These procedures took more time than simply issuing an edict (as in no fighting here; no running in the halls, chewing gum, using foul language, threatening another, and the like). The active involvement of every person in developing these tools for self-control assured that we had a standard that could balance being individuals with being capable of functioning successfully in a group. It eliminated the need for retribution and punishment imposed from outside. It held the promise that the errant behavior would not re-occur. The golden rule made ultimate sense when we'd all publicly acknowledged it. Power sharing was as much a part of our fabric as the three R's.

In time, when the pre-school kids grew to school age (5 years old), we ceased offering a three and four-year-old program. By law, children over the age of five can only be schooled in approved structures, buildings that meet certain health and safety codes. One mid-west U.S. restriction is that a building cannot be constructed of wood; it must be brick or metal. This being the case, we had to purchase the least-costly edifice on the market, a portable classroom. Washtenaw Community College, nearby, had a used one for sale. It wasn't long before we had to add another as well.

There were no grades levels in Clonlara, per se. The younger groups (called, appropriately, The Youngers) consisted of five to eight or nine year olds. Ten to twelve year olds comprised the Older Group until, around 1982, we added up to eighteen year olds. The groups are still named the Youngers, the Middles, and the Olders. Chronological age has less to do with which group a person belongs to than a readiness which is determined by the youngsters themselves and/or staff and parents in collaboration with the youngsters.

The rooms were set up in what became known as learning centers, mirroring the British Infant Schools of the day. A child could gravitate toward whatever interested her at the time and this ranged, for example, from dress-up clothes to construction blocks, from a comfortable reading station to a science experiment table, from telling time to measuring area and circumference. The focus, though, remained child's play in all its forms. For the older kids, whose brains had undergone the transition from concrete to abstract concepts, the discipline of lessons/classes was more eagerly welcomed.

Staff members, because they did not have to take center stage to address the entire group, were free to observe and to be of help as needed. One of the earliest observations we made, for example, was that youngsters who were the "only" children in their families tended to choose to socialize with others more often than not, while those with siblings often sought out solitary play.

Gretchen, for example, was the eldest in a family of three children. She held court in the sand box from her first day in pre-school until the Michigan weather forced us indoors in the fall. Inside, she set up elaborate town scenes with parks and buildings constructed with large wooden blocks; these became the dolls' domain. She pranced and danced her dolls through imaginary scenes for hours sometimes. Anyone who wandered into her sphere was welcomed and included by her as long as they chose to be there. As she got older, this pattern persisted but she added a counseling session for whomever seemed to bring a problem her way or whomever seemed to need a helping hand. She'd listen to another child's complaints or she'd watch for a spell while another child gazed off into space as though his mind was far afield. Almost imperceptibly, she'd summon them into her orbit. They respected her and confided in her. I mentally referred to this as Gretchen's Sandbox 101 class. It covered a span of three years until she was eight when she chose to spend time doing a wider variety of activities each day such as reading aloud to younger kids and setting up science experiments.

Other children, like Danny, age ten, "played" with math problems, his self-chosen hobby. Danny came to Clonlara from a conventional school where he was, in the words of his mother, "just wasting time being bored." His interest was with numbers. He brought a fifth-grade math textbook along with him and he pored over the pages daily. He'd copy problems, work through them, and bring the paper to me to correct for him; he made no errors in calculations for the chapters he covered. One day I gave him the teacher's manual with the answers given and he was shocked. That was forbidden. He was not allowed to see that; he was only the student. I pointed out that he'd know results quicker if he could correct his own work, but it took him a few days to dare to venture into that uncharted arena which he viewed as somehow illegal. He completed the fifth-grade text in a few months and then went on to each of the higher levels. By year's end, Danny had successfully worked his way through four grade level text books. If he made an error, he practiced that specific activity until he grasped it well and then moved on. He was one delighted—and delightful—learner. He was his own best math teacher and he reveled in that.

My own two children grew to take it for granted that I was both Mom and Teacher/Director of the school they frequented. During their early years (say, ages five to seven), I would hear reports from other kids, mostly as part of a discussion during a meeting called by a child or staff member. An aggrieved child would state that (usually) Chandra was bossy, saying that "my Mom owns this school, so you have to do" thus and such. By the time they got older, though, those comments seemed to disappear—or, at least, were not taken seriously enough to be reported to the group.

Paul Goodman advised parents: until a child is twelve years of age, she needs only to be surrounded by people who love her. No formal schooling. No adult-devised activities. Just a supportive environment in which he is free to explore and make sense of the world. His words rang true in the case of Chandra, who opted to leave Clonlara and attend conventional school not long after her twelfth birthday. On the first day at public school she came home with two arms full of heavy textbooks. "Look, Mom, they gave me all these books and if I finish them they'll give me more." She was jubilant. Her teacher was amazed and could hardly believe this child who was curious, who completed assignments, and who never tired of asking questions and learning. She had never been assigned a textbook before; she had not heard the same things over and over again until she burnt out on hearing them; and, most importantly of all, her brain had developed to create an apperceptive basis for formalized learning. She was/is our poster child for Paul Goodman's prescription, and also for Joseph Chilton Pearce's similar advice in *A Crack In the Cosmic Egg* and *Evolution's End*.

Fredda Clisham joined the staff as a volunteer several times a week. She became our resident Grandma. Among other things, she established "mail time." She devised an old-fashioned mailbox for the five to seven year olds' group and invited everyone, young and old, to post any messages they may have for anyone in the group. On a designated day and time, she'd place the mailbox front and center and ask whomever was willing to be the mailperson.

For the ones who lacked printing or writing skills, Fredda would serve as scribe (shades of Sylvia Ashton Warner) anytime during the week. Older kids helped, too, and they got caught up in the fun of watching someone open their letters. Everyone got a letter, since Fredda herself spent time jotting a (usually) short, relevant message to each child and staff member. Some had drawings in them in addition to words, and some had clippings from magazines pasted in them, even. It didn't take long for the game to catch on and for Mail Time to become a big hit.

Years later, Ellen, who had been a student in those years, told her parents and the class that this was how she learned to read. Fredda was surprised. "I am not a teacher," she said using a phrase that we were to hear countless times down the years after the Clonlara School Home Based Education Program began. Like Fredda, home educating parents proved that a certificate does not a teacher make! Fredda personified the parent/teacher who lovingly, openly shared with youngsters and provided a good model that kids could imitate.

Speaking of teachers… I asked A.S. Neill at Summerhill how he selected able staff members and his answer was that he looked for "people with loose stomachs." That was surely part of it, I found, but the task proved to be a daunting one. Men and woman who had gone through teachers' training at college or university and who held teaching certificates often came with the belief that they know how to teach, thank you, only to discover that youngsters weren't interested in being talked at or told things they weren't interested in. In that case, it was always the child who was at fault in the estimation of the teacher.

One man had taught in conventional schools for many years and had gone on to be a principal. He visited Clonlara for a day or so, and then he confided to me that he had hoped to spend some of his sabbatical time volunteering here but he wouldn't be doing that after all. Why? I asked. "Pat, I don't know how to teach," he said with look of helplessness. I explained to him that he could just share his interests with the kids. He was interested in fishing, but that "isn't a very valuable skill" for teaching school, he said. I assured him that it might just draw a good number of the youngsters, and, of course, it did. His was one of the most popular classes. Kids who hadn't yet developed reading skills were driven to learn so that they could read the magazines and books he brought from home with rods and flies and bait and boats.

Some veteran teachers had problems with listening to kids. Some expected parents to solve behavioral issues; their first recourse was to report a child's misbehavior to his parent at the end of a day. They had to learn that this behavior happened here in this place and, therefore, it had to be handled here in this place. Involving a third person who wasn't even present for the misdeed was pointless since the only one who could change the behavior was the child (with input from those who witnessed it and were affected by it).

Some who were adept at treating children with respect were highly critical of parents who, perhaps, were not as adept. They had to learn that parents are the unseen presence in every classroom in the world; that parents are consumers in this marketplace of education; and that parents, regardless of where they may stand on the continuum of understanding and guiding a child, are deserving of respect and patience in the same way that the child is.

Some mistook freedom for license, and abandoned common sense for permissiveness. Yes, a child is free to live and learn here; no, a child is not free to disrespect himself or others or damage materials that do not belong to him. "Your freedom ends where my nose begins," was the way one long-time staff member put it. John Holt made it clear in his many books that an adult ought not to be authoritarian, but must be authoritative. Treating one another and talking to one another the way a person would talk to a dear friend 21 year of age or older was the best description we came up with at Clonlara, and it did take practice to master.

Some are unsure about the word "structure." They assume that, because children have an equal say in what goes on in their lives, there is no structure in free schools. But, of course, there is structure. The question becomes who creates and imposes the structure that there is? A distant and absent Board? Policies written with no input from the people who are expected to follow them?

As the years passed and the ages of the children increased, we added more distant places to our itinerary, going where interests took us. A class on waterways led us to examine the Great Lakes starting from Lake Erie in the southwest to Lake Huron, through the Soo Locks to Lake Superior, and then down the west coast, Lake Michigan—a week of travel time.

In Dec. 1972, several parents and staff members drove two vans filled with seven to eleven year olds from Ann

Arbor to Cape Kennedy to witness the launch of the last manned space flight in the Apollo Series. We learned, once again, far more than the obvious space and science. Churches with schools (where we might spend the night) were hard to find in the preparation leading up to the trip. My practice was to telephone a school or church office to seek lodging. One conversation was an eye-opener for me: the Baptist pastor on the other end of the line listened to my plea and asked, "What kind of children are these (who attend Clonlara and will be traveling south)?"

It wasn't clear to me what he meant at first but after a moment I realized he was asking for the racial makeup of the group.

"They are mixed in both age and race," I replied.

"Well, in that case, we cannot accommodate your group," he said. Southern hospitality met its limits with that congregation.

We were very welcomed, however, to stay overnight at the Newman Center at Emory University in Atlanta, Georgia. We walked into a large conference room where men and women waited for us to shake off the dust of the day's trip so we could sit and enjoy the meal they had prepared for us—quite a surprise! A murmur grew at one end of the table as our youngsters and staff relished the glee of Juppie, Jason, and Vanessa as they noticed: every person in the welcoming committee was black like they are. We enjoyed an authentic Southern dinner, we were sent off the following morning with an equally hearty breakfast. Of the many lessons, we took away from this amazing experience, the main one, no doubt, was that in the end-of-day meeting a Clonlara staff member, a sociology student, cited demographic statistics: Caucasians are the numerical minority in the world.

When we filled the van with gas that afternoon, we saw three doors on the side of the gas station. Jim Montgomery (born and raised in Mississippi) explained that, prior to the 1965 Civil Rights Act, they had been labeled "men," "women," and "colored."

One trip that was an annual staple in our travel plans was to the National Coalition of Alternative Community Schools Conference hosted, generally, by a member school in some part of the U.S. For Clonlara students, staff and parents, it was a treat to be among many others who didn't require an explanation of what kind of a school we were and what we did each day. Member schools were by no means carbon copies of one another, but they did share a common allegiance to social justice issues and to empowering adults and youngsters to take control of their own lives\learning. Both staff and students from the various schools often planned during the conference for staff and student exchanges during the school year. Lasting friendships were formed. Conference sessions were "taught" by staff <u>and</u> students alike, as well as by invited outside speakers; it was participant-controlled in every possible way.

The farthest trip we took, and the longest to plan for, came about because of a new student's question about the name, Clonlara. Learning that it was the name of the village in Ireland where my own father had attended school when he was a child prompted us to locate it on a map and wonder. One long-time student suggested that we visit the "other" Clonlara and that launched big plans.

Twelve students and two staff members spent two weeks in the west of Ireland as guests of the parents and students of my father's Clonlara School, outside of Limerick.

It was as though we were walking back into history. We entered buildings that had been built several hundred years ago. We saw a replica of the boat that St. Brendan sailed to Newfoundland in long before the journeys of Columbus to North America's shores. We climbed the hills above Lough Derg, and attended a medieval feast at Bunratty Castle.

We also experienced today's Ireland. Peig Hurley, sixth-grade teacher at Salesian School in Limerick, invited us to spend a day as guests in her class. Her sixth-graders rolled out a veritable red carpet. One played the harp for us. A small group performed Irish dances while we watched in awe. Another told tales about early Ireland and recited poems. They all sang.

Peig invited us to perform anything at all for them if we'd like. That left us speechless. We hadn't prepared. Our Michael, age 15, saved the day by reciting an ode with such feeling and style that we all felt redeemed.

We spent recess period outside with all of the Salesian students. They taught us American visitors the game "Three Score" which originated in the 1800s. The founder of the Salesian Schools was an Italian priest named John Bosco. He was more popularly known as Don Bosco. The game stood the test of time was passed on to Clonlara's kids a century later. History was a living thing in Limerick and was presented to us joyfully in the same easy way as the ubiquitous tea and biscuits were.

People unfamiliar with the school often commented that the reason we could travel so much is that we were a *private* school—meaning that we charged high tuition, as in "elite." Staff members complained that they had to explain Clonlara's reality so many times that they sounded like a recording.

Travel with a group of youngsters is expensive, and there is no way that a small school like Clonlara could ever have managed to do it, especially since, at any given time, our student population consisted of about one-third low-income families. Except when traveling abroad, we rarely stayed in hotels or motels traveling, nor did we eat at restaurants. Instead, we carried all non-perishable food items with us, along with staples and cooking/eating utensils, and shopped for perishables along the way. Almost every school or church kitchen was made available to us, and our goal was to leave it as spotless as we had found it. We headed for campsites at various state and national parks, also. For the 20 years that Kitty worked at Clonlara, she made a large pot of her famous goulash so we could, at least, have a hot, home-cooked dinner the first night away. We held fundraisers for trip-taking, and we traveled on a shoestring.

Jim quietly became The Juggler of Finances. He had "robbing Peter to pay Paul" down to an art form. His parents, Reid and Ruby Montgomery, had helped Jim purchase rental properties in Ann Arbor as a means of supplementing our family income. These were the days when a person could purchase a house without needing a down payment, well before the ill-fated housing bubble of the 2000s. When Clonlara needed cash, Jim would first borrow from a bank, using our home and the rental houses as collateral. He would even sell one of the five properties we once held to underwrite the purchase of a temporary classroom unit or even meet a payroll.

Jim eschewed savings, per se, convinced that money ought to be thrown back onto the economy, always in motion. Other men climbed Mt. Everest. Jim commandeered credit. By the time the school was 30 years old, Jim had just one rental property remaining. That one was sold to help finance the new building.

We were listening to the evening news one night when we heard of a woman in Detroit who had a $100 a day drug habit. I expressed shock, disgust, and sympathy all intertwined. Jim shrugged his shoulders at me and said, "Pat, you have a $100 a day addiction, too. It's called Clonlara." If I didn't know by then how seriously he took his self-assumed role as Fundraiser-in Chief, I did in that moment. I counted our blessings.

Funding, in general, was and still is a major issue. There were times that we even had to ask staff members to cash their paychecks a week or more after they were issued because there was not a sufficient amount in the account to cover them. One way around this, it seemed to me early on, was to withhold a salary for my position as Director, a decision frowned upon by most business-minded people like bankers and several family members who then depended solely upon the income that Jim's position at the University of Michigan International Center brought in. It was a choice between closing Clonlara or accepting this harsh financial reality, and in my mind, the former wasn't even an option.

Had Clonlara not been a living-learning model of the sort it proved to be at every turn, perhaps my decision would have been different. But, the changes I observed in parents, kids, and staff, myself included, were enough to warrant severe thoughts and choices. Truth be told, I thought about the area of funding as little as I possibly could.

How far removed Clonlara's fare was from that of the Catholic school playground where my nun's rosary caused an administrator's uproar, or from that teachers' lounge at Mack public school where the veteran teacher castigated eager students-teachers' enthusiasm!

4
MOVING BEYOND CAMPUS

The writings of John Holt, especially his citing specific free schools in various parts of the country, went a long way toward spreading the word. Parents and students in the public schools began asking why they couldn't incorporate some of the novel practices of these small upstarts into their own daily operations. By 1972, for example, the words "alternative school" appeared for the first time in the U.S. Department of Education's search engine of the day, ERIC, the Educational Resource Information Center. It was not unusual for free school staff to receive invitations to speak to university classes or to give workshops at education conferences.

I accepted invitations to appear on the Phil Donahue Show on two different occasions, and one from John Chancellor's News Hour on national television, for example. Addressing classes at several universities and colleges also became the norm. It wasn't long before Clonlara was contacted by news outlets from other countries. An Australian crew asked to film a day in the life of Clonlara, and they broadcast the results in several former British Commonwealth countries.

"Omni" magazine did an extensive interview as part of their research on schools of the future. Clonlara, they concluded, exhibited the hallmarks of a school that heralded the future in education in the U.S. In the October 1985 issue of the magazine, the article, entitled, "77 Schools of the Future," appeared. "The school of the future will be no school at all," the article says. Citing John Holt's work, it points to Clonlara as a "center that provides support services" to people who need guidance and tailored assistance that aids and abets their own visions of what an education means.

So, in addition to growing by word of mouth, Clonlara became known at home and abroad. In this chapter, I will detail the relationship that we established with foreign educators and/or schools in four countries: Japan, India, Thailand, and Bermuda.

The story of Clonlara's close ties to Japan begins with a phone call I had from John Holt. I first met John at an alternative school conference in Athens, Ohio in 1970. He was the main speaker at the event; I was a workshop presenter. We compared notes at the end of the day, thus forming a collegial friendship. Thirteen years later, he phoned me from his office in Boston. He had a visitor, Yasushi Ohnuma, a reporter with the Hokkaido newspaper in Sapporo, Japan.

"I told him that I am no longer involved with schools since I am devoting my time to having people just teach their own. Since you are the head of the National Coalition of Alternative Community Schools (NCACS) and of Clonlara, I refer him to you," John explained. Then he gave the phone to Yasushi.

Yasushi was a reporter with the Hokkaido Shimbun (newspaper) and had been assigned the task of researching free schools like those John Holt wrote about in his many books. Japanese interest was fed by the publication of *Totto Chan, the Little Girl at the Window* written by Tetsuko Kuroyanagi, an internationally famous actress and talk show host. It was an autobiographical account of her early childhood. She was the little girl who, in kindergarten, exhibited her creativity so unabashedly that she frustrated her kindergarten teacher who threatened to expel Totto Chan from school.

Totto Chan left her assigned seat and stood at the window, and worse, she talked to the strolling musicians passing by who, in turn, regaled her with tunes and dances. Of course, the other children rushed to hear, disrupting the class. Totto Chan's mother couldn't bring herself to tell her vivacious five-year old that she failed kindergarten, so she withdrew Totto Chan and searched for another school. The year was 1941.

Tomoe Gakuin was the school they found, and a very unusual one it was. Its founder had purchased several old railroad cars, situated on unused railroad tracks outside the town. One was filled with water so that the kids and staff could enjoy swimming at any time of the day. There were no grades. Students had choices in what to study and when. They explored the world around them—fields, trees, and trails—learning from nature in unhurried, uninterrupted ways. A nearby shrine was one of their favorite spots.

Tetsuko reveled in the freedom and friendliness. She credits this early school experience with the unleashing of her artistic talents, leading her to her life's vocation.

Tomoe Gakuin was destroyed by bombs in 1945. Staff and students arranged to meet every year at the shrine nearby to keep its memory alive; it was at these gatherings that classmates encouraged Tetsuko to write her book.

Yasushi's editor sent him to find and chronicle as many similar schools in the U.S. as he could. I invited him to Clonlara and from here, he also visited schools in New York, Ohio, Colorado, New Mexico, and Florida before returning home to write and publish his series of thirteen articles. These caught the eye of Diakichi Suzuki, head of Ikkosha Publishing Company in Tokyo, who contracted with Yasushi to turn his articles into a book.

National schools in Japan at this time were bastions of pressure. Children attended six days a week for 280 days each year. Even their vacation times were prescribed by the schools—where they would go and what they would study. Children as young as three years of age competed with others for admission into prestigious national kindergartens. They sat for tests even at these young ages, and throughout elementary school, they learned by memorizing facts and undergoing testing. After attending regular school, on several days each week, they attended after-school school, called Juku. These are special private schools which offer lessons conducted after regular school hours, on weekends, and during school vacations. The word Juku, literally translated, means "cram schools." Here they engage in more rote memorization in preparation for the testing that they will have to undergo around the age of twelve which will determine whether students will be admitted to junior high school and college. This process is called, literally, "examination hell."

Competition and pressure exact a high toll from the human spirit. Children all too frequently react by becoming bullies to those less able—those who are shy, fat, thin, slow, or in any way different. Bullied students often become physically and mentally ill. They withdraw into themselves, blaming themselves. Some children have difficulty with the extremely strict regulations of schools, since every aspect of students' behavior is regulated, from the color of a district's uniforms to the length of a girl's skirt. Others are beset by the testing, testing, testing.

In one school, one twelve-year old girl timed her arrival to the school compound every day just in the nick of time to tag onto the line as it filed into the building. She was always last in line. A school administrator watched this performance over an extended period of time and was angered by the audacity of the girl. Seeing this as a form of rebellion and obstinacy, the administrator (whose job it was to press the hydraulic gate lever that closed the school grounds off from the street) decided to teach the girl a lesson. He pressed the lever to close the hydraulic fence just as the girl cleared it, giving the girl a shock and a warning. But she didn't learn well enough or she was determined to exert her individuality in this way. On the following day, the staff member pushed the lever too soon and the falling gate crushed the girl to death.

An eleven-year-old boy in Nagoya, remained on his futon for a full year, refusing in this thoroughly passive way to go to a place that offered him even more loneliness, isolation, and trauma than his choice did. Children as young as five choose suicide over school attendance. They believe that their inability to cope with the terror that school attendance causes them will cast a stigma on their family. On one of my trips to Japan, over the following years, I visited a ten-story hospital in Tokyo. Every floor held children who did not attend school; they were called "school refusers." The hospital's objective was to rehabilitate them so that they could return to the very schools that had sickened them.

It was against this backdrop that *Totto Chan* was published in 1981. The book broke publishing records; over 5 million copies were sold. The Japanese public sought answers.

Paradoxically, Japanese education was the envy of other countries. Japanese students regularly scored in the top five of the hundreds of countries in the world who participated in periodic international tests of science math, reading, and overall educational achievement[1].

Politicians and others in the United States, in particular, looked upon Japan's national system and its focus on testing as a model that might lift U.S. students' performances into that presumably rare stratosphere. So, those far removed from the lives of our children and intent upon using them as pawns in global competitive markets pushed and regulated schools to test, test, test; but parents and teachers—those closest to the process of

---

1   Trends in International Mathematics and Science Study: https://timss.bc.edu and National Center For Education Statistics (NCES) https://nces.ed.gov

living/learning—chose the opposite direction. Their goal was to assure that developing human beings have room to breathe and grow with minds, souls and spirits intact. They are convinced, with plenty of proof to back this up, that freedom to learn and to be self-directed is not, by any means, antithetical to educational achievement. The analogy of how kids learn to walk fits here: If we taught toddlers how to walk, they would, most likely, end up in wheel chairs.

But I digress. As I said, upon his return to Hokkaido, Yasushi submitted his findings in a series of thirteen articles on free school in the U.S. Diakichi Suzuki, head of the Ikkosha Publishing Company in Tokyo, asked Yasushi to put those schools into a book which Ikkosha published in 1984. After that, Mr. Suzuki invited me to address teachers, parents, professors, and the general public in six cities in various parts of Japan. That was the first of many such trips over the years. He also published several books about those trips, and one that I co-authored with Claire Korn, entitled *Free Schools, the Dream and the Reality* (1988).

At one talk, Keiko Okuchi, a teacher with many years of experience, posed a question: "Japan is not like the United States, she began. In order to start a school, a person must show that she has no fewer than 1000 students ready to enroll. All schools are under the Mombusho, the Minister of Education. How can we start a school?"

It was not difficult to ascertain that the question was directed as much to herself and to those around her as to me (who was still reeling at the seemingly insurmountable obstacles she faced). I borrowed then from a famous shoe maker and replied, "Just do it!"

Not even a year later—in 1985—Keiko, along with her colleague, Asukura Kageki, opened Tokyo Shure, a center primarily devoted to school refusers. It grew from one campus to four, in different parts of Tokyo, serving children ages 5through 18. In 1984, the school added a home school program, and in 1999, a university: Tokyo Shure University.

Tokyo Shure joined forces with other educational change proponents to create national associations like the Japan National Coalition of Alternative Community Schools and the Japan Free School Association. Members of these groups worked to effect changes in Japanese law. In 1992, they helped pass a law that assures government recognition of free schools. In 2016, their joint efforts resulted in another law being passed: The Ensuring Opportunity of Common Education Law, which extended recognition to home educated students.

Clonlara has maintained close ties with Japan throughout the span of the free school movement and the home school movement. Prior to the flowering of free schools in Japan, some families moved to the U.S. so that their children could enroll in Clonlara and other free schools. Michiyo and her (then) thirteen-year-old son, Taka, moved to Ann Arbor in the mid-Eighties, as did Konomi and her three children a few years later.

Having visitors from Japan became a common occurrence on campus. Reporters, teachers, parents, and students graced our halls. One teacher marveled at how natural and welcoming our students were. "Children here need to have only one face," he announced; then went on to explain. "Children who are under pressure must have one face for adults and another for their peers; here, they only need one face—the same for everyone."

The national television station, the NHK, sent a camera crew and reporter to film the school in action. Their gear alone almost filled one of our two portable classrooms. Then came the American National Broadcasting Company (NBC) right behind, filming the Japanese filming us.

Anne Thompson worked at Clonlara every summer when she spent time in the States, on leave from the Sri Atmananda Ashram in Kerala, India, where she lived the remainder of each year. Many Americans were part of the growing Ashram, along with people from Europe and India, and many had children. Anne was part of a group of them who hoped to open a school at the Ashram. Their efforts were successful.

Founded in 1987, it has grown to comprise three campuses, each with an enrollment of over 200 children. It is an affiliate of Clonlara School.

In the Lower Primary Section (ages 5 through 8), the children are free to decide which activities to attend and how to organize their own day according to their interests. By the Upper Primary Section (ages 8–11), the children engage in group projects that require a longer attention span. High School (ages 12–14) and Plus-Two (ages 15–17) sections offer students a choice. They can pursue preparation for the external board examinations—the International General Certificate of Secondary Education (ICSE) and Diploma Program (ISC/IB), similar to the British model, or they can pursue a Clonlara diploma. Sri Atmananda Memorial School's graduates have gone on to higher learning in India and abroad.

Piphob Udomittipong and Rajjani Thongchai, educators from Thailand, attended the National Coalition of Alternative Community Schools Conference at Antioch College in Yellow Springs, Ohio in 2000. Rajjani and her husband, Phiphop Thongchai founded Moo Baan Dek—The Children's Village—in 1979. It is a home, a school, and a community for orphans and other at-risk children, located on the River Kwai, in Kanchanaburi, in the west of Thailand.

The children in Moo Baan Dek come from difficult backgrounds. Many come from very poor families, broken homes and abusive environments. It is not unusual for children to be sold into the sex trade by members of their own families who use the money to buy food or farm animals.

Phiphop and Rajjani, inspired by A. S. Neill, combined his philosophy with local culture and Buddhist dharma. They designed the school so that the children live close to nature in a place where they are free to develop trusting relationships with compassionate adults, a democratic community where healing and learning occur.

I visited Moo Baan Dek on two separate occasions. On the first trip, I met with teachers, parents, and students there, and I lectured at universities in Bangkok and Changmai (2000). The second trip was to join the founders of Moo Baan Dek at a series of meetings with government officials in Bangkok. The purpose was to raise awareness of non-coercive education and lobby for changes in Thai education law.

In conventional schools there, teachers were permitted by law to use corporal punishment in the classrooms, a common practice. The accent was on training children, not engaging them. Thanks to the fact that Moo Baan Dek was well-known in Thailand and beyond, and thanks to the untiring efforts of its founders and staff, the Thai legislature enacted The Educational Act in 2005; it allowed citizens an active participation in school governance matters.

Merle Swan Williams, educator, author, and poet, founded the Adult Education School (AES) in Hamilton, Bermuda in 1958. As its name implies, AES was designed to serve adults who—for one reason or another—had not graduated high school. Classes are kept small so as to allow for flexible scheduling and a personalized approach.

Merle later developed an affiliate relationship with Clonlara to initiate yet another program in Bermuda for high school drop-outs and kids at risk of dropping out. It combined tutoring by Merle and her staff of Bermuda teachers with home school work. Students had the option of creating their own path to graduation or following the usual Bermuda high school route. They graduated with Clonlara's diploma, and many went on to colleges and universities in Bermuda and the U.S.

Over the 50 years that Clonlara grew and developed, we added programs and services that allowed the philosophy and practices of the campus school to be shared with others who needed them. Each had its own signature, and even its own name/descriptor. There were sister-schools and satellites, and affiliates all tucked in to the general concept of transporting the work we did each day to others who wanted to do similarly. Some requested guidance on how to start; others required help with complying with their regional or national regulations; still others wanted fuller involvement so as to have their students actually participate in our campus program from a distance. The result, overall, served to be as enriching for parents, students, and staff in Ann Arbor as for the parents, students, and staff in those far-flung places of the globe.

Needless to say, these contacts resulted in close, personal bonds and in deep organizational ties. They also underscore the universality of the yearning to empower people to nurture their own instincts and to strike a balance between living as an individual while also contributing to the communities we each inhabit.

5
EXTENDING INTO HOMES

One spring day we had visitors to Clonlara: a couple from St. Joseph, Michigan and their eight-year-old son, Richard. After they had taken a tour and observed, had talked to some students, a parent of one student, and to me. I asked whether they were planning on moving to Ann Arbor since they lived over 150 miles away. No, they said; they came seeking help in order to teach Richard at home. They would have the benefit of being attached to a functioning school but he would not attend. It was 1978. Up until then, neither I nor they had ever heard of a "home school."

At the end of the day, after further discussion, we established the support and materials that family would need to make this idea a success. We laid plans to communicate regularly and to assess the arrangement periodically. At first blush, it seemed like an odd thing to be doing, but on further reflection I realized how similar this was to what I myself had done: I had never been an administrator before; had never started a school; and yet I was free to do these things with support from others who shared my vision. So, who was I to disagree with the choice that these earnest, searching, eager parents wanted to make? Was this not the message at Clonlara's core?

Here was an opportunity to extend what we did every day on campus to parents and kids who may never even visit us in Ann Arbor but who'd be connected nonetheless. Not to mention the long-term potential it posed for our having a way to fund the campus school without having to sell apples at the University of Michigan football stadium or hot dogs at the annual Ann Arbor Art Fairs.

The visit from the St. Joseph family set into motion a series of events which prompted a major change at Clonlara and even bigger changes in state law that are chronicled in Chapter 6.

It wasn't long before word spread, all by word of mouth; we had requests from parents from other parts of Michigan and from other states as well. The second year thirty families were enrolled, and the numbers grew each year. Finally, Clonlara had generated a way to fundraise that capitalized on what we actually did every day while providing a service almost identical to that of the campus, day school.

Parents were asked to cite their reasons for home educating on the enrollment application form. Some indicated that they simply wanted to live and learn together without the constrictions that accompany institutional/government schools; they became known as "unschoolers" over time, and our staff dubbed them "rugged individualists." One thing they had in common was that they viewed education/learning as completely separate from schools and schooling; they embraced the fact that the ability to make connections constitutes learning and that this is best done through mindful involvement with real things, an essential part of everyday situations. Living is learning and humans learn all the time.

Some families cited religious reasons for choosing to keep their children at home. The Bible mandates in Deuteronomy 11: 18-20,

> *"Lay up these my words in your hearts and minds, and hang them for a sign on your hands, and place them between your eyes. Teach your children that they meditate on them, when thou sittest in thy house, and when thou walkest on the way, and when thou liest down and risest up."*

Pastors in many congregations exhorted parents to remove their children from public schools using this admonition. These biblically-inspired people became the largest and most organized of the recognizable groups of home schooling families, probably because rugged individualists, by definition, did not ordinarily form groups. These families cited their intention to follow a Biblically-based approach right down to their choices of curriculum, books and other materials.

Other families chose to walk a line between using traditional paraphernalia (textbooks, workbooks, testing, etc.) and child-initiated activities. Still others did not classify their reasons as any mentioned so far. They stated a desire to "reclaim their children as a whole family again" or "avoid starting a child" on a conventional school path in the first place, or they quoted Margaret Mead's explanation that her "grandmother wanted to be sure she got a good education so she taught her at home."

Clonlara, by developing its extension program—Clonlara School Home Based Education Program (CSHBEP)—in 1979 welcomed all, regardless of their reasons, regardless of their race, creed or lack thereof, regardless of where they lived or what level their students were at prior to enrolling. The desire to home educate and a willingness to accept the conditions of enrollment were sufficient. The number of enrollees grew annually as more and more parents opted to keep their families together during the childhood years. As more staff members were added, more office space was needed, so a second portable classroom was purchased to house the campus students and staff; CSHBEP used one of the two original frame houses, while the campus inhabited the other plus the two tin can units. In no time, the second program was larger than the first; the tale was wagging the proverbial dog.

Upon enrollment in CSHBEP, a family was/is assigned a Clonlara staff member as teacher-advisor/mentor. Teachers who had formerly taught in our campus day school made excellent advisors since they had an understanding and appreciation of noncoercive practices and communications; they could ease the concerns of parents and students and share with them the value of focusing first and foremost on human relationships. Later on, parents of Clonlara graduates served in these positions as well. Advisors met regularly with one another to ponder commonly-asked questions and share workable solutions.

Completion of the registration form constituted a compact between Clonlara and the family. Parents and students agreed to:

1) follow an approach to living and learning which was thoughtfully and deliberately

2) tailored to the interests, needs, and abilities of each child;

3) describe and define that approach; maintain as much contact with their assigned mentor as they needed;

4) abide by the rules and regulations in their state of residence; and

5) inform Clonlara of any changes in their program.

Clonlara agreed to:

1) assign a teacher/advisor who would shepherd the family's progress and maintain students' cumulative file folders;

2) maintain as much (or as little) contact as parents and students requested;

3) maintain timely communications;

4) assist parents with all means of assuring compliance with the rules and regulations of the state of residence; and

5) assist in procuring any books or materials a family may want (maps, manipulative materials, books, tests, etc.).

Clonlara hosted an annual Home Based Education Conference, open to all but geared particularly to enrollees: parents, students, grandparents, neighbors, and friends. Staff members took advantage of this three-day time to meet their students and parents face-to-face and to get a fuller picture of the families' programs.

The enrollment packet sent to each family included a curriculum for the family's use but they were also encouraged to employ any design for their program that they chose as long as this design was made known to their teacher-advisor so that s/he could give appropriate guidance and counseling. This arrangement allowed, say, Muslim, Jewish, Catholic, Christians of various denominations, and Jehovah's Witness families the space to incorporate the tenets of their beliefs into their days.

Families were free to choose whatever books and materials they wished, and these could be purchased by Clonlara for them (since companies—for many years—refused to deal directly with mere parents). Contact between family and advisor occurred through letters in the mail (pre-electronics), phone, sometimes (but not often) in-person visits; later, the parties kept in touch by email and Internet.

Parents and students were free to contact their mentors at any time, whether for a specific need or just to touch base. Families could expect to receive guidance and counseling on all aspects of a family's life, not just academic work. In fact, parents soon discovered that reading, writing, and arithmetic were the least of the issues they faced.

Almost all who applied were accepted, but occasionally there were inquiries and registration forms that presented questions such that admission was denied. One parent, for example, intended to use home schooling as a weapon against his estranged wife. Another intended to remove a teen from conventional school without so much as consulting him. These instances were rare, though, probably because such parents saw the futility of paying hundreds of dollars in tuition when they had no intention of following an established set of expectations.

As in the campus school, kids who had attended conventional school before home educating—especially those who were teens and had been in school for a length of time—needed a time to de-compress when they transferred to CSHBEP. Advisors repeatedly heard stories of kids who read comic books for the first several weeks or just sacked out on the couch for some days rather than dig right in to "school" work. Parents worried that this behavior would last into an indeterminate future. Then what would happen? The student would be throwing away an opportunity. Parents were relieved to learn that it takes time for a student to shift from being in a place where their opinions are not sought, where they are not trusted, and where they are not expected to even have interests, let alone follow them and nurture them, to a place where they could take control over their own lives, follow their interests, and trust their instincts again.

Students who had taken lessons outside of school—such as dance, instrument or vocal music—and those who were immersed already in so-called extra-curricular activities—such as equestrian studies, Olympic and other sports, travel, chess tournaments—were grateful to learn that these activities "counted" as school and that they were free to pursue them wholeheartedly. Lending support to parents was a prime role for the staff who learned that listening is a far better tool for assisting than asking questions is. Conversely, while listening, they sought to hear the question behind the question.

For example, a parent might fret," How long does it take for a teen to *like* academic subjects?" Translated, that often meant "How can I get her to open a textbook?" It took time for both parent and youngster to appreciate that textbooks work better as reference books, quite expensive reference books at that. They are much better replaced by *real* books like those found in libraries. It took even longer for many to re-direct the question to themselves in an attempt to discover why they were equating learning with schooling and the trappings of school.

Often, a parent just had to be encouraged to talk to his/her child in the same way that s/he would talk to a friend who is twenty-one years of age or older, regardless of the child's actual age. The default position was to continue to use declarative and imperative sentences with a youngster (ordering, demanding, correcting, explaining) instead of simply stating the facts as one sees them—such as "It seems like you have given up on the school-related work you once had to do." Not passing judgment, faulting, blaming. Being willing to trust the child to work through her transition from compulsory schooling to learning, the way she did from birth to school.

So far, thirty thousand students have been served in CSHBEP. Here are a few random examples of enrollees over the years. Their actual names are not used in the interest of preserving privacy.

Kathleen and Jonathan never attended institutional school. They both, at an early age, took an interest in playing tennis, and by the time they were twelve and ten years old respectively, they showed sufficient promise to warrant a coach of their own. The family became immersed in the game and wrapped other interests around a schedule that took them to tournaments and competitions in various parts of the country. Mom's work was the family, and Dad was a writer, so it wasn't too much of a stretch to live out of their motor home when they were on the tennis circuit. They dubbed the large motor home "The Blue Goose" as a nod to Howard Hughes' Spruce Goose. The number and variety of traveling games they invented was a thing of legend, and some of the less complicated ones were adopted by Clonlara campus school travelers on their numerous junkets. Neither Kathleen nor Jonathan became professional tennis players; they attended college after Clonlara and Kathleen chose a career as an economist and Jonathon became a civil engineer.

Maxine, age 11, had been labeled a special needs student in her public school in western New York state. One teacher told her parents that Maxine "would never be able to care for herself" so they "ought to be looking for an institution" that would accept her. They chose to home educate her instead. By engaging Maxine in ordinary activities that she was able to perform, either easily or by stretching and practicing, they gave her the platform she needed to succeed in small, then larger things. She gained confidence again and, around age 16, showed a knack for seeing what needed to be done and quietly stepping up to do it: setting up chairs at church gatherings, helping to serve food at homeless shelters, stringing decorations for conference parties, and the like. Eventually, she developed a cooking talent even to the point where she created her own menus. She volunteered at a nursing home that served elderly and infirm patients for several years before being offered a paying job in the cafeteria. She lived in a group home not far from where she worked. Without parents who refused to accept a cruel directive, Maxine might never have grown to be a contributing, active woman, happy in her own skin.

Not all students see the point of going to college or university; some, like David, resolutely avoided that traditional route. He was raised on a farm in Nebraska, tending domesticated animals—cows, horses, donkeys, all manner of fowl, cats, dogs, and household pets. Feeding, grooming, medicating them when they came down with an illness—all of it. He explained that his approach to the natural process of growing/leaving a family to step out on one's own was to turn his back on domesticated animals and take an interest in animals in the wild. At age 16 he contacted Columbia University to find out how he might join a group of researchers who lived and operated in the Yukon Territory studying moose, deer, birds, and the like. Since he was not a student and had no intention of even going to a university, his chances appeared slim until the person who interviewed him realized the store of knowledge and experience that he brought with him. Without having to be taught, he understood what creatures are about and how they ought to be handled; consequently, he was accepted as a member of the team, ahead of undergraduate and graduate students who had put their names on a list long before but who lacked the expertise that David was raised with. About 83% of Clonlara graduates do choose to go on to colleges and universities, though, and others, like Rachel, whose story is below, go into businesses of their own. Still others enter the armed services.

Mollie, a girl from a rural area of Ohio, rode into her commencement ceremony one June on horseback. We had risked the weather to hold graduation on the spacious grounds of Clonlara, allowing for such an auspicious entry. She had been engaged in equestrian pursuits throughout her childhood and this was but a step forward toward a career in riding competitions, breeding, and teaching.

Roger attended his graduation in his full clown regalia; early on he exhibited a showmanship and humor, along with a sense of organization that propelled him to complete clown school.

Rachel attended both public and private schools in Chicago until she reached the freshman year of high school and was expelled as a juvenile delinquent. Her behavior ranged from stealing to hanging out on the streets. Through counseling, she and her Mother reconnected and tentatively chose home education as a way for her to finish high school. It was Rachel who contacted her Clonlara advisor regularly and, over time, she clung to the idea of re-discovering herself and her interests as the lifeline that brought her to graduation in 2014. She and her Mother, when her name was announced, came forward to accept her diploma. Her Mother took the microphone, turned toward her daughter, a slightly-built 17-year-old with a lush head of hair dyed purple on the left side and orange on the right. "Rachel," she said, "I am so very proud of you.

Your journey through this whole homeschooling experience has been most remarkable. You walked away from those influences in your young life that would have destroyed you and sought out challenges that re-awakened your spirit. I was your single-parent Mom who struggled to keep us in rent, food, and clothing until you discovered your strengths in practical math and business. You now own a 50-unit apartment building in downtown Chicago and are closing a deal on a high rise, multi-use building nearby. But even better than this, I got my daughter back and you have your sanity and dignity again." In that room of some 400 people, a pin could have dropped.

Graduation at Clonlara is always the time for such intimate sharing amongst kids and adults who get it: learning is too precious a thing to hand off to well-meaning people of any stripe. It is a personal endeavor in which the teacher within is allowed to step forward and flourish. It flowers from the unique history of an individual from birth on. It fulfills the promise of that magnetic pull (vocation) which every human being harbors within his soul. It is a constant, never-ending process that has, far too often, no connection whatsoever to schools and schooling.

Graduating students—like home educating families taken as a whole—differ from one another in every way—race, creed (or none), family demographics, and country of residence—but they do have some things in common. They share an experience of knowing that living and learning are inseparable. Their singular strengths and capabilities deserve far more attention and nurturance than some impersonal, board of education- conceived curriculum. They appreciate and accept that they have a purpose and a mission in life. The graduation ceremony presents an opportunity for students and their parents, relatives, friends and teachers to address the assembly, explaining the journey that their lives have been on until that point and spelling out the hopes and plans they have for the days to come.

Several Clonlara graduations took place during the annual conferences we held for a number of years; most occur in the multi-purpose room of our school. Helen Hegener attended one in the Eighties and in the subsequent edition of Home Education Magazine she wrote: "If you go to a Clonlara graduation, be sure to take a box of Kleenex tissues along."

Now, one might be led to conclude from reading these accounts that home education was and is a highly successful endeavor. The parents and students who opt to engage in it agree that it is. Even families who try home educating but find, for whatever reason, it is not for them, can discontinue it without major upheavals in their lives and routines. There are other ways to educate. Home education is a small operation, even for large families. That allows the operation to turn on a dime, so to speak, in ways that institutions cannot.

The Clonlara staff who served families know that it is successful because they are in contact with the folks who are doing it. They keep annotated records. They chart the growth and development of the home school program. The general public knows it because they see with their own eyes the progress that individual home educated kids have made.

But home education engendered a very different, oppositional response from public school officials—from the local level right up to state departments of education—during the Eighties and Nineties. Here are just a few of the encounters families were forced to endure.

Superintendents were the first public school officials who reacted to parents' choices. Most addressed an instance of home educating by citing the compulsory schooling law and ordered the parent to cease and desist. If that failed, they handed the case over to their truant officers.

Some, though, attempted to understand why a parent chose to ignore the school as a place worthy of allegiance. These latter usually asked for in-person meetings where they'd try to discover what prompted refusal to send children to school. For example, a superintendent in Highland, Indiana, met with Pam, a parent of five children. I drove down to attend the meeting with her because parents, in general, are seldom asked to meet with the district superintendent, and because I was aware of the fact that Pam was then seven months pregnant with her sixth child.

Pam explained her family's choice to use their home rather than school. The superintendent responded, "I must tell you that I am committed to public education; my life and my hopes are wrapped up in public schooling, what you are doing causes me grave concern. If you succeed, and if others join you, it could spell the end to public schooling." I pointed out that, in his relatively large school district, there was but one family who had made this choice. By the time we finished the meeting, he acknowledged that we were talking about two very different types of education: institutionally-based and home-based.

The two approaches have very little in common, and this was made clear throughout our meeting.

Another superintendent, in Bullock Creek, Michigan summoned a single-parent mother of three boys, all former high school students in his district. She was understandably reluctant to meet with him, concerned that her answers could somehow jeopardize their home education. I offered to attend the early morning meeting with her. His greeting to her was, "I didn't know you were bringing anyone with you." This, as he led us into his office where five other men sat waiting; they were teachers who taught or counseled her sons. "She didn't know you had invited her to a meeting with six men, either," I pointed out as we took our seats.

She quietly circulated copies of her sons' reports cards issued at mid-term; each card listed failing grades in every subject area for each boy. Never had she been contacted about this, not by a teacher, principal, counselor, or the superintendent. She let it be known that whatever they would be able to accomplish at home in the time remaining of their school years would be better than what had been done in school. To his credit, the superintendent sincerely apologized to her that his district had done poorly for her family, and he wished her well.

Though they rarely admitted it publicly, most superintendents feared the potentially sizeable loss of state money to their districts should home schooling become a movement.

Truant officers, another group of public school officials who figured prominently in the drama, handled home education with cut and dried edicts: the law is the law, other people aren't keeping their kids out of the schools (so you shouldn't either), put them into school or face court action. Period. Some, in collusion with school administrators, reported parents to state social service agencies, claiming "failure to send children to school" or "child abuse and neglect." Their aim was to pass the problem to the more visible and active Michigan Department of Social Services (DSS). Their goal was thwarted, however, because the DSS soon became aware that it was being pulled into a political fight between the schools and families who were not guilty of abuse and neglect and who were not failing to educate their children. The Department issued an order in the mid-Eighties stating that home education did not fall under the purview of their social workers unless actual child abuse was occurring. Even so, they were bound to at least investigate any complaint, and this alone posed a serious threat to families.

Finally, the truant officers' organization—the Michigan Pupil Accounting and Attendance Association (MPAAA)—appealed to the Michigan Department of Education for advice and guidance on how to handle a growing number of parents opting out. They got nowhere. The rest of *that* story can be found in Chapter 6.

Society, generally, regarded home education as fanatical, chosen by people who had an axe to grind and used their children as tools. Grandparents and in-laws were quick to question a parent's decision to educate at home—and were often the hardest to convince. Neighbors and friends of the parents and kids also took issue, as did fellow churchgoers, scout troop leaders, and on and on. Most often, the underlying suspicion was that this family, by reason of home educating, was casting aspersion upon every other family's choice to do the ordinary thing. Either that or they were crazy.

Public school officials in various parts of the country did not respond to home education in the negative ways that those in Michigan and in many of the States east of the Mississippi River did. In California, Oregon, and Washington, for example, school officials scurried to find ways to include the home schooled even though they were not in daily physical attendance at the schools. Public schools in those states set up oversight programs designed to serve the parents and students who opted for home. They set up centers where parents could find books and materials and receive the guidance of teachers and counselors if they so desired. In some areas, school sports teams welcomed the participation of home schoolers. These efforts were based upon the condition that the absent students could be figured into the equation when head count time came twice each year. A pro-rated amount would then still appear in the public school district's allocation of state tax monies.

In parts of Colorado, home school families were invited to submit requests to their public school districts to receive money for field trip travel, books, tests, and other materials. This assured that the local school district, having processed and overseen the requests for funds, would receive their due in form of tax monies as well.

Not all families took part in these arrangements. Families who chose to avoid school often did so because the parents' own past experiences in schools repelled them, or they were distrustful of school run by the government. For these and any number of similar ones, they declined offers of funding.

Home, of course, had traditionally been the only venue for a child's learning and growing into adulthood. Schools were the new kids on the block, historically speaking. The resurgence of home schooling in the late twentieth century provoked some serious drama in a world where people forgot that past, and where parents handed over the responsibilities of rearing their children. Fortunately, time heals. It took about twenty years or so before calm was restored.

Parents who choose to home school today seldom worry about being summoned to court by irate authorities. Home schooled students have gone on to become fully-contributing members of society. They can be found in every walk of life. Now that a few decades have passed, society in general accepts home education as a bona fide method of education. The gargantuan amount of energy, effort and expense that it took to arrive at this point was well spent.

Clonlara's programs—both its campus, day school and its home based education services—are recognized all over the world by parents and by conventional school authorities, even college admissions officers. Home schooling is legal in almost every country of the world.

6

CLONLARA V. MICHIGAN DEPARTMENT OF EDUCATION

In the autumn of 1979, months after the family from St. Joseph, Michigan enrolled in Clonlara School as stay-at-home learners, I received a telephone call from Paul Turnbull of the Michigan Department of Education (MDE) in Lansing. "I understand that you have a student enrolled in your school who does not attend, he said. Is this correct?"

"Yes," I replied.

"Well, we could shut your school down for this," he said.

"Would that make you happy, Mr Turnbull? I asked with a smile in my voice.

"I hope you are not starting a program for people like this," he said.

I was not smiling when I hung up the phone. I understood down to my bones that his threat was not an idle one. I headed for the University of Michigan law library, a mile away. What does education law state? What rights does this family have? What rights does Clonlara have? There had to be answers; perhaps the Michigan Code of Law would provide them.

Provide them it did! In essence, Michigan law stated that all children must attend public school unless they are exempted by attending another school, on the condition that such school have a program similar to the public school. And there was a footnote: In 1955 the State Attorney General rendered an opinion that *educating a child at home* was permissible under Public Act 302.

Armed with fact, I made an appointment with Mr. Turnbull in Lansing. I took along a mock-up of the brochure we would use to launch the Clonlara School Home Based Education Program (1979). I had taken him up on what seemed an excellent idea. This time, Mr. Phelps, second in command to the State Superintendent, Philip Runkel, joined the meeting.

"Are you telling us that parents who do not even have a teaching certificate can teach their own children?" he scoffed.

"Yes," I answered; "in just the same way that many people who teach in public schools all over this State do."[1]

This was the first in a long line of such meetings

---

[1] In Detroit, as just one example, when public schools couldn't find certificated teachers, they hired people who had at least 90 college credit hours in any subject area. The MDE then issued a Temporary Teaching Permit. It made the person a certificated teacher for one year only (renewable annually) and only for that particular school. That differentiated it from the certificate held by the majority of teachers who are required to complete college/university classes and a degree, and who can take their certificate to a school of their choosing. Of course, this was not published information; it was an in-house solution.

that I—and, as time went by, home education advocates from all over the state—attended. Each session focused on the responses that the MDE had to this phenomenon of home education, continuing to grow in popularity (except at MDE).

The MDE soon issued a statement declaring that home schools are non-public schools and, as such, they are subject to the same requirements made of all other Michigan non-public schools. That sounded fair on the face of it, but it contained three flagrant flaws:

1) All Michigan non-public schools were not treated equally;[2]

2) The regulations MDE attached to their statement were markedly different from the ones they sent to nonpublic schools;[3] and

3) The stated requirements actually contradicted one another[4].

---

[2] In 1986, the Michigan Supreme Court ruled in *Baptist Church v Department of Education* that nonpublic schools need not abide by the MDE's regulations if, for religious reasons, the opposed using a state certificated teacher.

Numerous private schools throughout the state made a point of using only Masters' or Ph.D. graduates in a specific subject area rather than employ state certificated teachers.

[3] Clonlara had been a non-public school for (then) 17 years and had been filing the appropriate annual forms with the MDE; a simple comparison of two quite different sets of requirements told sordid tale of unequal expectations.

[4] To cite but one contradiction: parents had to "use the services of a state certificated teacher inside the home for 180 days of the year." A later listing stated that since teachers would be doing one-on-one tutoring, "it may not be necessary for the teacher to be present in the home for a full 180 days."

Nonpublic schools were required to hire teachers who possessed valid Michigan teaching certificates. One elementary school teacher, however, could have as many as 35 pupils in one grade; a secondary school teacher might teach as many as 120 students per day in rotating classes. If 35 unrelated children could be taught by one certificated teacher, why did a tutor for one or two children have to possess a certificate? Why could Christian school and elite private school children who shared a teacher with many others be taught by non-certificated teachers while home school students could not? Would teachers at Interlochen Arts Academy, Cranbrook School, or Roeper School now be forced to have a state teaching credential?[5] How could parents of limited means be able to teach their own youngsters if they had to hire a certificated teacher?

Why was the MDE requiring parents to have a teacher for 180 days? This matter had already gone before the courts and been decided in 1988 in *Houghton Lake Community Schools v MDE*. In this case, this northern Michigan public school district refused to make up the substantial number of snow days its schools were closed in the prior winter (1987-88). The State then denied the district its per pupil funding. The court found that the School Aid Act of 1979 provided only a financial "carrot" to school districts who provided 180 days of instruction, but "there was no clear legal duty" to do so; the district received its funding minus the prorated amount for the snow days.

---

5 In *Kentucky v. Rudasill*, the Kentucky Supreme Court ruled the state could not require use of state-approved teachers and textbooks in nonpublic schools. The U.S. Supreme Court, without comment, refused to review that decision.

Non-public schools do not receive tax monies from the state; the Michigan Constitution expressly forbids it. The number of days these schools are in session each year is determined by each school itself; nevertheless, MDE regulations for parents required 180 days.

Finally, if a nonpublic school failed to abide by the regulations of the MDE, it had to be given an administrative hearing with all of the time allotments before being taken to court and possibly facing closure. Parents who home schooled, conversely, were frequently summoned to court as soon as a local district discovered that their children were not attending public schools.

In summary: the MDE's attempt to regulate home schools was, at best, fraught with contradictions, hastily-made regulations, vagueness, and inconsistencies; at worst, it was bureaucratic maneuvering masquerading as law.

All of this played out against a background of parents and school-age children learning at home, though a growing number were forced to conceal the fact from school officials and even from neighbors. Many stayed inside during regular school hours so as not to provoke questions. Clonlara instructed parents to let anyone who inquired know about their enrollment in the school program and to give our telephone number to any inquirer. Not surprisingly, I began to receive calls from truant officers, especially since we taught parents how to comply with the law and how to proclaim their rights. For a few years, enrollment with Clonlara was a major protection.

Clare, a mother of four who ranged in age from five months to eight years, phoned. Her home was in a rural area upstate; her husband had left for work that morning a usual, but shortly afterwards a sheriff's car drove into her driveway and two men, both in plainclothes stepped onto her porch. The children were still in bed. She virtually whispered into the phone, "Pat, they are rapping at the door but I am not going to answer."

I walked her through the procedure: yes, she was right not to answer the door to two men she never saw before who arrived with no advance notice. Yes, she had the right not to be interrupted by strangers. No, she should not answer the knocking. I told her further to hang up, call the sheriff's department to make certain that ununiformed men had been sent, and explain that she was not going to speak with anyone at this time.

Then I phoned the sheriff's office and was patched through to an irate man, who was standing at Clare's front door that very moment. He demanded to know why I agreed to this belligerence; all he wanted to do was check for negligence. I assured him that, with the courtesy of an appointment, when both parents could be present, he'd be able to do just that.

Besides, I added, would he want his sister or daughter—given the same circumstances—to allow two strangers into their rural homes? Or the teacher of his child to be interrupted, summoned from her classroom to speak to unannounced strangers in the hallway? Reason prevailed. The district made proper contact with the family by mail, an appointment was mutually arranged, and the family was left to educate without interference thereafter.

So many parents in the Toledo, Ohio area were summarily taken to court for failure to send children to school that the court clerk who had to process all of these cases finally decided to cut to the chase. When a parent appeared in the court, summons in hand, the clerk handed them Clonlara's phone number and told them that if they wanted a positive outcome, they should seek Clonlara's help.

School personnel, in general, were so accustomed to calling the shots and being obeyed without question that they bristled at the prospect of seeing "mere" parents acting independently. One father of a farming family in southern Michigan was jailed for teaching the couple's seven-year-old. His wife appealed to Raymond Moore, noted author and home school advocate who then resided on the west coast. Raymond, in turn, phoned me and encouraged me to assist the family, though they were not enrolled in CSHBEP. Even so, the Judge was willing to listen to me, and after interviewing both parents, he declared them not guilty as charged. The parents, reunited, returned home to their child, hearth and fields.

In the early 1980s, home school groups began to form with the purpose of spreading factual information and support for parents who opted to education from home rather than to use schools. Religiously-oriented home school groups, in particular, formed and flourished all over the U.S.; the major one in Michigan was the Information Network for Christian Homes (INCH). Some of their members served in the state legislature, so the Lansing meetings grew more frequent and now stretched to include addressing legislators. The number of participants in meetings with Department of Education functionaries also increased.

INCH representatives and I met again and again with

Mr. Runkel and/or his staff in Lansing over a period of six years' time. We appealed to them to stop the destructive actions of local school officials as they waged war against parents who opted out of public schools.

During one meeting in Lansing in March 1985, we representatives took issue with their latest iteration of the Department's home school requirements, point by point. When we got to the matter of having a state certificated teacher inside the home every day, I posed this question to the State Superintendent: "If the Department demands that a family hire a teacher to be in the home every day for 180 days, how many hours of the day must that teacher be present?" Mr Runkel and his associate exchanged impatient glances; then he replied, "We're not telling you."

His level of arrogance reflected precisely the proprietary attitudes that far too many school officials exhibited toward parents and students on a regular, daily basis: We own you and you will do as you are told without question. His brash demeanor and his vulgar choice of words effectively ended the meeting.

By the time I arrived home–an hour and a half later—I was convinced that we were never going to find common ground or reach an agreement with these officials, try as we might; it was useless to continue getting nowhere.

Jim and I commiserated over dinner. The injustice of it all was incredible. People are sitting in jail, accused of crimes, hiding their children when the school bus passes, cowering in fear of having their children taken away. And the Superintendent who has the power to change this doesn't even care. Child abuse and neglect? Let me tell you who's guilty of child abuse and neglect, Mr. Superintendent.

It is surely the school officials at, for example, Dexter High School in the town next to Ann Arbor. In the final week of his high school years, they denied an 18 year old boy his diploma and the right to walk down the aisle for graduation. He'd spent twelve years in that district. His grades proved that he was an excellent student; his teachers affirmed that his behavior had been laudable throughout; and he had been a track star in his final years, winning trophies for the team. That was all wiped away with the Principal's decision. The boy's mortal sin was that he had walked into the gym in his street shoes three days before he was to graduate, though he knew the rules and had always abided by them before.

His parents pleaded with the Principal, the school Board, and the Superintendent but the gauntlet had been thrown down and no one was willing to reverse the decision. THAT is child abuse and neglect.

The teacher who told Lisa, age 6, that she "would never read"—she is guilty of abuse and neglect. The age of learning to read differs for every person. Any teacher worth his salt knows that. It's age three for some and age twelve for others, and if all else fails, even adults can learn to read. But Lisa was convinced that her case was hopeless. She bore the snickers of her peers when the teacher called on her to try to read aloud to the class. She suffered the torments of bullying because the other kids picked up on the teacher's criticism. Every day, her head bowed closer to her chest as she gazed out at her world through her long, brown tresses, defeated. THAT is abuse and neglect.

And, the people like those at the Department of Education, people who pay more heed to their paperwork than they do to the individuals whose lives are affected by each policy and regulation they put forward, by each hoop they create for the minions to jump through. They are guilty of child abuse and neglect. It's a crying shame!

"There's only one thing that these people in Lansing will understand," I concluded. They are the ones who ought to be sued; they are the ones who are guilty. Jim agreed. The fact that we had no funds for filing suit in court never came up. If money stands between you and the thing you want most, then you do not want it very much, I concluded. That thought accompanied me in the search for an attorney who might take the case.

Ed Nagel, the Santa Fe Community School Director, and a friend from the National Coalition of Alternative Community Schools organization, traveled to Michigan to assist me with the search. The finest lawyer in town for matters of rights and justice, I was told by other lawyers, was Kurt Berggren. Ed and I visited Kurt. He agreed to take the case.

Clonlara, Inc. v State Board of Education was filed in 1985 in District Court in Lansing. It claimed that the MDE does not have the power to make rules; that power belongs to the legislature, and therefore MDE's regulation of home schooling was illegal. The judge agreed. The MDE appealed.

The Michigan Court of Appeals agreed with the District Court's decision. The MDE appealed.

In May of 1993, the Michigan Supreme Court[6] ruled

---

6 Three home school-related cases had been wending their way through state courts—the Bennett case, the DeJonge case, and

that the MDE home school regulations (called "compliance procedures") "are interpretive statements that do not have the force of law." Case closed.

After 14 years of fighting the Michigan Department of Education over its arbitrary, illegal actions toward home schoolers, the chapter was closed and victory was won, but any trust that ordinary citizens could have in government was gravely eroded. Paul Bricker, a home schooling father of three and an attorney very knowledgeable about the workings of bureaucracies, came to the rescue. He advised me to make an appointment with members of the Michigan Board of Education and to appear before the Board to suggest ways that we might engage in dialogue rather than fight. Paul set up meetings, counseled and advised me and the others who joined efforts with us, and the process began.

The upshot was that a nonpublic school advisory committee was established to facilitate communication on a relatively regular basis. The Michigan Nonpublic School Advisory Committee began meeting in 1994. Since home schools are nonpublic schools in the eyes of the state, representatives from brick and mortar school associations joined leaders of several home school groups to form the committee. Religious, non-denominational, proprietary, alternative and home school groups were all welcome—a mix of schoolers and non-schoolers.

The group met periodically over the next year or two, but it became obvious that the brick and mortar school representatives already had communications with the

---

Clonlara's case. The Supreme Court combined the cases and rendered a single opinion.

Board of Education. These lines of communication had been set years before, and they were sufficient to satisfy the schools' needs. It was the home school representatives who had heretofore lacked any lines of communication with the bureaucrats who governed their choices. Home educating issues, therefore, filled practically every committee agenda. Soon, the school representatives stopped coming to the meetings. The committee faded into oblivion after about a year and a half, but methods of communication had been established, and the option for direct contact is more possible now than it had ever been in the past.

Individual parents, too, had learned a critical civics lesson; each must stay abreast of what is happening in state bureaucracies. Each must take responsibility to be aware of and, to the extent possible, involved in the political process. That is what democracy looks like!

7
CSHBEP'S OVERSEAS VENTURES

Clonlara's home based program journeyed abroad in much the same way as its campus school had done. Although the issues that parents and students in distant lands faced were slightly different than those of their U. S. counterparts, they were substantially the same. The States had no premium on authorities who did not hesitate to pull rank on the people they purported to serve (aka administer to).

In this chapter, I will share the stories of home schoolers in Sweden, Spain, France and Germany—all places where families opted to enroll in Clonlara. We—they and Clonlara—traversed the world of laws, child-rearing and unschooling hand in hand: distant learners and fully-functioning, independent school together.

Like clockwork, every year for five years, Magnus Drysen and Maria Berkestam received a summons to appear in court in their native Katrineholm, Sweden. The local school superintendent regularly filed suit against them because their three children, Viktoria, Aurelia, and Aron, didn't attend school. This was in the mid-90s. Every year, they received a fine, and every year they refused to pay the fine based on principle. (The fine was for "failure to educate.")

One late summer, they enrolled with Clonlara School Home Based Education Program. When I learned of their annual plight, I decided to go to Sweden in September to meet with the Superintendent in person. That proved to be a Kafkaesque episode. He welcomed me as though I were an old friend and explained in some length how much he favored parents' right to make the choice to educate wherever they thought best. At first, I wondered if I had the right person, but the sign on his door bore his name.

After we exchanged greetings, he took me on a tour of the school then back to his office where we engaged in discussions—one professional educator to another— which ranged from the inordinately long period of time it takes schools to reform to Sweden's neutrality during WWI. Interesting, but not the reason I had traveled from the States to meet with him. I changed the subject then.

Oh, that? Well, they have a right to make a choice, he assured me. "I fully support a family's right to choose what is best for their children," he said. He made no explanation of how this statement and his annual actions against the family veered so vehemently. Anyone hearing this amicable exchange could have surmised that he and I were old buddies just taking the time to share views and opinions. On the tour of the school, he had pointed out the sad fact that the very same desks and chalkboards which we saw before us were the ones that had been there when he himself attended that school years ago. He bemoaned how little has changed over the years, not only in furniture but in approach and too many other practices as well.

He said that he fully approves of home schooling, and he was glad that a school such as Clonlara exists to assist people. I had gotten over my initial shock by this time, and I decided to take him at his word, bizarre though it was. I gave him several Clonlara brochures and encouraged him to share his enlightened views of parents' choice with other Swedish school officials who may have home school students in their districts (called kommuns). He said he'd be glad to do that. Surreal, indeed!

My hosts, on the other hand, were far removed from Kafka's fiction. They were, and are, vibrant, realistic, involved parents who open their lives to their children and include them in decisions that affect the family. In return, the children were interested, enthusiastic, and involved. They reflected the quiet determination of their parents; they mirrored the same respect for others, the same willingness to make things happen, that they observed in Magnus and Maria.

Together they planned family trips outside of Sweden, often for six months of a year. Magnus took off work and they caravanned around Europe. They often met and visited with other home educating families, residents of the countries they visited. They learned Spanish and French to add to their Swedish and English. They moved as a unit, learning all the time.

One year, they traveled the world and recorded their adventures in a book, *Extended World Travel*. It's on their Facebook page and in blogs that they've done over the years. Google: Magnus Drysen. Over the years, the family sponsored annual home education conferences on their farm in Katrineholm, bringing together families from various parts of Europe, the Scandinavian Peninsula, and the Middle East.

Two Spanish families, one from Barcelona and one from Almeria, enrolled in Clonlara (CSHBEP) in 1999. Both were educating elementary- age children. The family in Almeria was summoned to court by local and regional school authorities and for two weeks "La Voz de Almeria" newspaper carried feature articles about the court proceedings. "Student Lives 6000 Kilometers From His School" blared one headline; "Boy of Eight Years Studies Only On the Internet," said another.

Misunderstandings abounded. The boy's parents tried to set the record straight; they explained to the judge what they were doing and how. The judge ended the case by personally interviewing the boy. Then he told the parents, "Whatever you are doing, continue to do it. Your child is an intelligent, creative boy, and your choice of education for him is working very well."

Xavier Ala, father of the family from Barcelona, drove to Almeria where I met with all parties. To my surprise and delight, Xavier had already translated Clonlara's brochure and materials into Spanish and was circulating them far and wide. He became the first Director of Clonlara Espana.

Jennifer Fandard and her family reside in France. Jennifer, her husband, and their two teen-agers live in Villers Agron Aiguizy, France. They enrolled in CSHBEP so that the children would receive a high school diploma from a school, a document that could accompany them to a college in the States, Canada, England or France.

I met with the family at Biocultura conference in Madrid, Spain in 2002. Jennifer was a presenter in one of the education workshops. She explained to the audience of home educators and other interested people the three categories of home education extant across Europe at the time.

1) Countries where the law supported parents' choice to use home as the base of their children's education—like France, Wales, and England;

2) Countries where the state monitors home education—like France, Belgium, Luxembourg, Austria, and Switzerland; and

3) Countries where home education was permitted under special circumstances—like Greece and The Netherlands.

She pointed out that home education is forbidden in Germany, and for that reason, several German families had relocated to the village where the Fandards live in France. Jennifer helped spread information about home educating and about Clonlara's program in France, and in the various European countries in which she frequently spoke and shared her own experiences.

The first time I was invited to Germany was to address parents and educators at a National Association of Natural Learning (Bundesverband Naturlich Lernin) conference. The group had been founded by Anke Casper-Jurgens, and in 2002, they hosted a gathering near Dusseldorf.

Among the participants were German parents who wanted desperately to educate their own children at home; many had their own small children with them. A 400-year-old law stood in their way. It was roundly ignored until the time of Hitler. He seized upon it as a way to indoctrinate youngsters for his own political ends. Germany is the only country in the world where such a law exists and is enforced.

I explained that when U.S. families reside in states where compulsory attendance laws stand in the way, parents form groups of like-minded people and work to change the laws. In the meantime, many parents keep their children home, acting in civil disobedience.

"We Germans are a people who revere obedience to law," one young father said.

'We cannot ignore it."

"Is this the same country that produced Martin Luther, the sixteenth Century priest who nailed his Ninety-Six Theses to the door of All Saint's Cathedral in Wittenberg in defiance of the Pope and the Catholic theology of the day?" I asked. But, alas, I was at a loss to think of another example—except, perhaps, Hildegard von Bingen.

I was forced to agree with a German lawyer who was also a presenter at the conference. He said, "It is not necessarily the 400-year-old law that is the major hurdle here. It is the cultural mindset of the German people."

In 2004, Karen Kern, a German parent, arranged for me to do a speaking tour of Germany, from Frankfurt to Hamburg, from Lake Charlotte to Leipzig, from Berlin to Dresden and points in between. Karen and her husband, Matthei, had successfully home educated their three sons. When they were threatened with German law, their eldest teen-age son took it upon himself to seek approval from the

United Nations Court of Human Rights. He maintained that it was his right and the right of his parents to choose the type of education he would have. He cited the United Nations Charter on children's rights. He won the case.

Meeting so many parents and students, all wishing to be free to teach their own without government intrusion and interference—in precisely the way that families in many other countries of the world were doing—increased my hope that this could be accomplished, even in this last, stubborn society.

Still, to this day, parents, students, educators, and reformers in Germany are toiling to make that happen. Still, to this day, Clonlara serves families in Germany who teach their own. Some few have made agreements with local and regional education authorities, but this is not universally done. German parents often cross the borders to take up residence in a neighboring country so that they can home school—just like parents everywhere who do what they must for the benefit of their bairn. The struggle goes on.

Clonlara School has served home educating families in over 60 countries so far. The most heartening thing for me was to meet parents and kids at conferences in the Netherlands, Ireland, Spain, Germany and Japan. They were united in their hopes, dreams and life choices to those at similar conferences in Michigan, New York, Ohio, Pennsylvania, Missouri, Washington, Oregon and California.

Just as these families are cut from the same cloth, so, too, do they rejoice in the results of their efforts. Their children, having been educated in the crucible of the family, go on to pursue lives as adults who are contributing members of their communities, happy in their own skin.

Almost to a family, they had read John Holt's books about how children learn and about the value of home schooling. Educators, parents, and students in schools read John's earlier books on how schools and the adults in them should strive to be. Wherever in the world I traveled, I found that John Holt was present there in his writings. Many of his books were translated into every language, from Thai to French, Japanese to Spanish, and many another in between. His work is widely-known in the United States and beyond. He is well loved for his immense contribution.

ROOTS OF CHANGE AND SUPPORT STRUCTURES

Free schools—places where youngsters are treated like the thinking, intelligent human beings they are—were not new to the Sixties. The ideas that propel them are as old as Socrates and have been present throughout recorded history. Over the last 300 years there have been writers, philosophers, educators, scientists, medical doctors, psychiatrists, biologists, artists, anthropologists, and reformers who have promoted learning in natural, unhurried, humanitarian ways.

Sandy Hurst and I chose a selection of names for several workshops we co-presented at different conferences from time to time that charted the path of the past, listing numerous movers and shakers whose works we had read or had referred to others. Sandy had chaired the NCACS Teacher Education Program for many years; she was familiar with the things that student teachers in university classes were being taught about alternative education (precious little, as it turned out). It occurred to us that a listing of the names and dates that these people lived and contributed might be valuable to student teachers, historians, and others. The following is the sum and substance of what we discovered. Some had started schools and were themselves educators in their day. Others thought about and wrote about educational theory. All paved the way

The first time that we presented our findings, one young woman, a recent graduate of an East Coast college of education, announced that she had "never seen such a compilation" and thought that she had been cheated. The listing follows:

Jean-Jacques Rousseau (1712 – 1778), a French philosopher whose work influenced the French Revolution, wrote *On Education*. He said that children are naturally good, and he believed that people develop through various stages, and different forms of education are appropriate to each stage. He emphasized the importance of setting up an environment where children develop ideas on their own to make sense of the world in our own way. People must be encouraged to reason their way through to their own conclusions—they should not rely on the authority of the teacher.

Johann Heinrich Pestalozzi (1746 - 1827), a Swiss educational reformer, took up Rousseau's ideas and explored how they might be developed and implemented. His early experiments in education (at Neuhof) ran into difficulties but he persisted and what became known as the "Pestalozzi Method" came to fruition in his school at Yverdon, established in 1805. Instead of dealing with words, he argued, children should learn through activity. They should be free to pursue their own interests and draw their own conclusions. He said: "I wish to wrest education from the outworn order of doddering old teaching hacks as well as from the new-fangled order of cheap, artificial teaching tricks, and entrust it to the eternal powers of nature herself, to the light which God has kindled and kept alive in the hearts of fathers and mothers, to the interests of parents who desire their children grow up in favor with God and with men." (Pestalozzi quoted in Silber 1965)

Friedrich Froebel (1782 – 1852), a German educator, and a student of Pestalozzi, is known as the founder of the first kindergarten (garden of the children). He saw this as a place where children can observe and interact with nature, a place where they themselves can grow and develop in freedom from arbitrary political and social imperatives.

Leo Tolstoy (1828 – 1910), a Russian known as one of the greatest writers of all time, founded thirteen schools for his serfs' children, based on the principles he described in his 1862 essay "The School at Yasnaya Polyana." Tolstoy's educational experiments were short-lived, partly due to harassment by the Tsarist secret police. However, as a direct forerunner to A. S. Neill's Summerhill School, the school at Yasnaya Polyana can justifiably claim to be the first example of a coherent theory of democratic education.

Charlotte Mason (1842 – 1923), a British educator, author of numerous books, and founder of The Parents' Education Union and a teacher education college in Amberside, England presented a system of education that reflected her strong Christian beliefs. Jesus said, "Let the little children come to me, and do not hinder them, for the kingdom of heaven belongs to such as these." (Matthew, 19:14.) Charlotte Mason believed that children were born persons and should be respected as such. Her work was re-introduced to the home school world through the publication of Susan Schaeffer Macaulay's *For the Children's Sake* (1984).

John Dewey (1859 - 1952), an American philosopher, psychologist and educational reformer, believed that, in order to learn, children must be active; schooling, he said, is unnecessarily long and restrictive. His idea was that children came to school to do things and live in a community where they can have real, guided experiences which foster their capacity to contribute to society.

Maria Montessori (1870 - 1952), an Italian physician, believed that each child is born with a unique potential to be revealed, rather than as a "blank slate" waiting to be written upon. She founded the schools that bear her name and that have been established all over the world. "Play is the work of the child," she said. The role of the teacher is to create the environment conducive to assuring this critical activity.

Rudolf Steiner (1861 – 1925), an Austrian philosopher, social reformer, and architect said, "To be free is to be able to think one's own thoughts, not the thoughts of a teacher or of society but thoughts generated by one's own deepest, most original, most essential and spiritual self." Steiner founded the Waldorf Schools, so named because of the funding for them came from the Waldorf Astoria Tobacco Company.

Alexander Sutherland Neill (1883 - 1973) a Scottish progressive educator and author founded Summerhill

School in Leiston, England (1921). His school attracted both admiration and criticism from around the world. It is an emblem of child-centered education. Self-governance was a central idea to Summerhill and is, perhaps, its most fundamental feature. A weekly general meeting was held where the school's rules were established and disputes were Every member of the community—staff and student alike—had a single vote. Summerhill flourishes still under the guidance of Neill's daughter, Zoe Redhead.

Jean Piaget (1896-1980) was a biologist who originally studied mollusks but, when his first child was born, he moved into the study of the development of children's understanding processes. He observed his own child's behavior and then enlarged his study to include many children of varying ages, observing them and talking and listening to them while they played.

Sylvia Ashton-Warner (1908 – 1984), a New Zealand writer, poet and educator, spent many years teaching Maori children, using stimulating and often pioneering techniques which are documented in her book, *Teacher*. She created a teaching style that engaged a child in his own reading and writing so that his words and ideas came from his own essence, and, consequently, were vital and important to him.

Paul Goodman (1911 – 1972), an American novelist, playwright, poet and psychotherapist, was best known as a social critic. He wrote *Growing Up Absurd* and *The Community of Scholars*. He pointed out the fact that education occurs outside of schools and despite one's having to attend school. He argued that it is in schools and from the mass media, rather than at home or from their friends, that children learn that "life is inevitably routine, depersonalized, venally graded; that it is best to toe the mark and shut up; that there is no place for spontaneity." Trained in schools, children go on to the same quality of jobs, culture and politics. This is education... "socializing to national norms and regimenting to the nation's needs."

Goodman recommended that education be transferred into factories, museums, parks, department stores, etc., where the students can be active participants. Ideally, schools would be small discussion groups of no more than twenty individuals, using whatever environment is relevant to the interest of the group. He advocated for the elimination of compulsory schooling because it "retards and impedes the students' ability to learn."

Haim G. Ginott (1922 – 1973), an Israeli teacher, a child psychologist, and a psychotherapist, pioneered techniques for conversing with children that are still taught today. His book, *Between Parent and Child*, stayed on the best seller list for over a year. It outlines specific practices, based on good communication principles, that guide parents and teachers in living with children in mutual respect and dignity. He echoed the belief of A.S. Neill: we teach children from the neck up, ignoring their feelings. He appealed to parents to reverse this cycle, to listen empathetically.

John Holt (1923 – 1985), an American author and educator, a proponent of homeschooling, specifically unschooling. He was a proponent of progressive schools in the 1960s. His voluminous writings include: *How Children Learn, How Children Fail, The Underachieving School, What Do I Do Monday?* and *Teach Your Own*... and many more.

George Dennison (1925 —1987), an American novelist and short-story author is best known for *The Lives of Children*, his account of the First Street School founded by his wife, Mabel Chrystie. After serving in the U.S. Navy during World War II, he attended the New School for Social Research on the GI Bill, and took graduate courses at New York University.

Although he devoted himself primarily to his art, Dennison also taught school for a number of years, at all levels from preschool to high school. He trained at the New York Institute for Gestalt Therapy with Paul Goodman and later worked with severely disturbed children as a lay therapist and teacher. As an educator, he promoted the idea that relationships, not instruction, promoted real learning. Schools needed to be places where freedom of choice created the trust that allows for a full relationship between teachers and students. These ideas were considered radical because they questioned compulsory attendance and the focus on controlling student behavior by the use of rewards and punishment which interferes with relationship. Schools should be small, familial places, he said. In the late Sixties George and his wife moved to rural Maine, where they raised three children.

Joseph Chilton Pearce (1926 – 2016), an American author of a number of books on human development and child development, and is best known for his books, *The Crack in the Cosmic Egg*, *The Magical Child*, *The Bond of Power: Meditation and Wholeness*, and *Evolution's End*. He emphasized the necessity of play throughout childhood; without it, the human brain does not develop to its maximum potential.

The movers and shakers cited above are the giants upon whose proverbial shoulders we stand. And, there are contemporary authors and activists whose work has contributed to the growth and spread of both the free school/alternative school movement and the home education movement. I have been fortunate to know a few of them personally and have been inspired by their words and their work. Among them are Chris Mercagliano, Mary Leue, Jerry Mintz, Sandy Hurst, Lu Vorys, Steve Molnar, Herb Kohl, Marvin Garzia, Jesse Mumm, Ed Nagel, Jack Wuest, Herb Snitzer, Dr. Robert Skenes, Jeannie Douha, Sally Carless, Dayle Bethel, Phil Moore, Pat Farenga and Jonathan Kozol… to mention a few.

In addition to individuals, certain groups—associations, councils, conferences, and societies—have provided pillars of support to free schools and home schools. They are platforms upon which schools and families build networking webs to enrich their programs and to strengthen one another in any number of ways. Below is a descriptive listing of those which the staff, students and parents at Clonlara found particularly helpful.

The New Schools Exchange (NSE) was the first nationally-circulated newsletter for and about free schools. It grew out of the first New Schools Conference in Menlo Park, California, March 1969. Harvey Haber, conference leader, convened hundreds of community based school representatives from the small schools that sprung up just in that decade. The schools each sought to provide an alternative to the public education system, which was increasingly criticized for large, factory-like schools with unwieldy class sizes, impersonal atmospheres, authoritarian methods of discipline, and outmoded curricula. Their philosophies and practices varied, but most were small, private and innovative institutions organized on a grass roots level. They generally based their practices on ideas of children's freedom, self-governance and social justice.

Haber, impressed by the size of the conference attendance, took the microphone and said, "I declare this a movement, and it is." He went on to set up NSE as a clearinghouse for information on free schools and published a newsletter and directories that linked schools, programs, and individuals in North America and abroad.

Bill and Grace Harwood assumed leadership of this vital nexus in 1973, moving operations first to Paris, Ohio and then to Pettigrew, Arkansas where they combined subsistence agriculture and community living with NSE work. The final newsletter was published in 1978. Bill donated all publications, correspondence, directories, and related documentation to the Yale University Library where it is available as "New Schools Exchange (Inc) Records.[1] It was the NSE newsletter that publicized the annual conferences hosted by a Chicago based organization, the Alternative Schools Network, in the early Seventies.

The NSE was a lifeline for all at Clonlara. It was something apart from us, but it reflected what others in distant places were doing that so closely resembled what we were about. "Out of the box" loves company!

Bill Harwood visited in 1974 and mentioned that a survey of these schools was begging to be done. If only we had the time, he lamented. Coincidentally, I was searching

---

[1] New Schools Exchange (Inc) Records, **drs.library.yale.edu**.

for a topic for my Ph.D. thesis. Bingo! We had a fit. I arranged to travel out to his community farm in Arkansas to copy the data I would need to contact the various schools and programs. That turned into a cross-country trek for the eight to twelve years old group at Clonlara, two teachers, and me. The thesis was published by the same University Microfilms Company that was supplying end reels of paper that we used at Clonlara. It all wove together! In 1978, the Harwoods donated all documents amassed by NSE to the Yale Library.

The Alternative Schools Network (ASN) has been directed by Jack Wuest from its inception in 1973 onwards. Jack is Executive Director still today. Its Chicago conferences brought together parents, teachers and administrators from the U.S., Canada, South America, and farther afield. Anyone seeking to change outdated educational institutions was welcome.

The contribution that ASN made to the free school movement and the home education movement was and is momentous. Its conferences, for example, provided valuable opportunities for networking across the country and beyond. They allowed otherwise isolated educators, parents and students the singular chance to meet and learn from one another and from leaders in the two movements.

Paulo Friere was a frequent speaker as were George Dennison, Herb Kohl and Jonathan Kozol (for example). During the May 1977 ASN conference, representatives of several alternative schools developed the idea of forming a national group of alternative schools.

Today, ASN focuses on helping dropouts, eliminating joblessness, and educating teachers for inner-city school work—not only in Chicago, but all over the country. A large part of its efforts goes into educating politicians and other policy-makers about the actual people behind the statistics they see every day.

ASN played a big role in the life of Clonlara. It was through our regular attendance at annual conferences that we met Lu Vorys, Ed Nagel, and Dorothy Werner and many more people who were engaged in teaching and administering free schools in other states. It was there, too, that the idea to start a national free school organization was planted and took root. There, we met staff from Pedro Albisu Campos School and the Puerto Rican Community Center of Chicago, institutions that figured prominently in the lives of Clonlara's students and staff, particularly for field trips and staff exchanges. We were much the richer for that.

The National Coalition of Alternative Community Schools (NCACS), as mentioned above, grew out of ASN meetings amongst the free school staff in attendance. Following one conference, I bemoaned what had become an annual refrain among the free school staff whom I met at ASN conferences: we ought to start a national association of free schools. Each year, when we returned home, the daily order of our lives took command and we didn't follow through with these hopes. It occurred to me that someone had to take action or the idea would remain forever on the drawing board. So, I phoned Lu Vorys, founder of Metropolitan School in Columbus, Ohio and we hatched a plan. She and I returned to Chicago within the week. We asked Jack Wuest for help, namely, for contact information on the various small schools represented at ASN conferences. Jack pointed us to his files; we collected dozens of addresses. Before heading for home, we composed a letter of invitation to a planning meeting set in Ann Arbor for just one month later (June 1977).

Representatives from Urban City School in Cleveland, Ohio, Santa Fe Community School in New Mexico, Metropolitan School in Columbus, Ohio, and soon-to-be schools in New York and Pennsylvania attended. The NCACS was born. The principles upon which the NCACS was built were defined in its by-laws:

The aim of the NCACS is threefold –

1) empowering youngsters and adults to actively and collectively direct their own lives;

2) placing the control of education in the hands of the learners-students, parents, teachers; and

3) developing tools and skills to work for social justice.

The organization provided its member schools, interested individuals, and later, home schools a place for sharing ideas and resources. Most of the schools were located in communities that had no other similar entity within their borders, so staff and students felt isolated, surrounded by those who chose the customary route: conventional schools. The NCACS published a bi-monthly newsletter which featured information on working free schools, and it published a directory of such schools.

The NCACS held annual conferences which were unique in the educational field; these proved to be the organization's greatest contribution. Conferences were usually hosted by a member school/program. Each conference included segments designed by and for students; some were fully designed by students—both youth and adult events—and students served as conveners of the annual membership meeting as well. In other words, the same sort of democracy-in-action that was the hallmark of each separate school in its daily operations governed the goings-on at the conferences.

Schools—staff members and students—participated in teacher and student exchanges between schools were not uncommon, and were often arranged at NCACS conferences. Naturally, the matter of how to raise funds for the schools was a perennial issue, as was the matter of prospective staff finding schools and vice versa. Most of the schools and programs were independent/non-public, but a few were public schools—like the Ithaca, New York Alternative Community School founded by Dave Lehman. (Upon his retirement, it was re-named the Lehman Alternative Community School.)

These gatherings allowed kids to "grow up with" other free school students from every part of the U.S. and, later, from Japan, Canada, Mexico, and Columbia. The close personal influence that this organization had upon so many of the schools' students can be summed up by an episode that happened in the early Nineties: Ellen, a Clonlara student and a graduate of Community High School in Ann Arbor, was admitted to Amherst College in Massachusetts. She traveled east to a new place only to be gripped by a feeling of isolation, knowing not a single soul on campus. As she lugged her suitcases into the dorm, she heard her name being called. It was Josh, new to Amherst from his home in New Mexico. The two of them had met every year at the NCACS conferences. "It was like having a family member right there with me," Ellen said.

But students were not the only ones drawn together from otherwise unconnected places. Nat Needle, a staff member at Clonlara during the Nineties met Mihoko Wakabayashi, a staff member at Tokyo Shure in Japan, at an annual NCACS conference. They developed a relationship which continued over the distance of thousands of miles. Together, they arranged the one-month school exchange between students and staff of the two schools: two weeks in Japan for Clonlara's group and two weeks in Michigan for Tokyo Shure's. Nat and Mihoko married and spent time in both countries before settling in Salem, Massachusetts, where Nat had started an alternative school some years before coming to Ann Arbor, and where they now have a spiritual community and a Japanese weaving business.

In 1983, the NCACS responded to an invitation to send a representative to the Federal Department of Education's newly-formed Nonpublic School Advisory Committee which met periodically to review projects that, from time to time, involved nonpublic schools. The National Center for Educational Statistics, in particular, sought input for the design of its numerous surveys and studies of all schools in the country, nonpublic as well as public. Leaders of Catholic, Christian, Episcopalian, Lutheran, Quaker, Adventist, Hebrew, non-denominational, Montessori, Waldorf, and for-profit schools comprised the committee. (This committee still meets, at least once a year.)

The NCACS dissolved in 2014, mainly because its membership numbers had declined, and because other associations offered similar, and greater, services to alternative schools.

Home Education Magazine (HEM) was started by Mark and Helen Hegener in 1983 out of their home in Tonasket, Washington. It advocated for unschooling, the living and learning family lifestyle that Helen herself had experienced as a child in Alaska, along with her younger brother and sister. She and her husband continued the practice, unschooling their five children.

HEM was a mainstay of support for families, for state advocacy groups, and for Clonlara enrollees throughout its all-too-brief existence. It provided a forum for parents and kids to submit their daily experiences as home schoolers, and it helped them weave a web of support networks.

HEM did not shy away from political themes by any means. In 1991, in a special report, it published "Homeschool Freedoms At Risk" (May-June issue). Mark and Helen wrote:

> Homeschooling is one of the most influential grassroots movements our generation has seen coming together. We are, by the very act of homeschooling, making a strong social and political statement. The lessons which homeschooling families are learning are causing ripples in every corner of this nation. People are sitting

up and taking notice of this new alternative and the amazing effect it is generating in the way we look at children, learning, and the family.

The edition catalogued the "exclusive hierarchies" represented by "Home School Legal Defense Association Court Report", the Christians Home Education Associations spawned by Greg Harris's book, *The Christian Home School* and by "Teaching Home Magazine. These publications advanced the notion that there is only one way to homeschool, and that was/is tied to a narrow range of social and political support. The sense of community that was being lost in this damaging process was the basis for HEM's alarm.[2]

CSHBEP parents, students, and staff used HEM religiously. It gave us a networking platform, numerous topics to mull over in staff meetings and discussions, and a newsletter that we could circulate among our enrollees to accentuate a point and/or to share the glee of home educating. In one issue, HEM contained a letter from a reader that cited the work of the NCACS; that proved to be a source of discussion among NCACS member schools and a theme of its conferences for a few years to come. HEM touched us in many ways. It ceased publication in the mid-Nineties.

---

2 The divisions caused between homeschool advocates, home school families, and the groups they formed is a chapter for a different book.

The Alternative Education Resource Organization (AERO) was founded by Jerry Mintz in 1989, and he still holds the position of Executive Director today. Jerry had founded Shaker Mountain School in Vermont in 1968 and directed it for the next seventeen years. He served as the first executive director of the NCACS (1985-88). Jerry is, first and foremost, a networker writ large. He has traveled the world promoting alternative, democratic schools. Assisting others in starting such schools is one of his main goals when he is not writing books and articles about alternative education, hosting annual conferences, operating an alternative education teacher training program and publishing newsletters.

AERO's goal is to advance student-driven, learner-centered approaches to education. It is the primary hub of communications and support for educational alternatives around the world, and includes in its membership both schools and individuals. Montessori and Waldorf schools, both public and nonpublic schools-of-choice and schools for at-risk students, democratic schools and homeschools—all are numbered among the membership of AERO. Its mission is to help create an education revolution to make learner-centered education available to everyone.

International Democratic Education Conference (IDEC) was founded by several well-known activists in the free school movement. Yaacov Hecht, an internationally distinguished leader and founder of The Democratic School in Hadera, Israel launched IDEC in 1993. He first convened a meeting at Hadera School, inviting about a dozen people whom he knew to be involved in democratic education.

One of the people who responded was David Gribble, one of a trio of founders of Sands School in Ashburton, England (1987). Another was Jerry Mintz. These three were the primary shapers of this international conference.

Each year, the conference is organized by educators at alternative schools or by some similar group. The organizers plan every aspect of the conference from the length of it, the program and the cost to attendees. Youngsters always play a large role in its execution. So far, IDEC has taken place in a different country each year. Venues have included countries located on each of the continents, except Antarctica.

IDEC limits its work to being a conference. It has no office, no staff, per se, and issues no newsletter. Its aim is to unite people from all over the globe who are already involved in their own pursuits. It serves as their connecting link, allowing them to meet one another and to share globally.

The place of AERO in the annals of Clonlara is legendary and it, no doubt, will be for many years to come. Through Jerry Mintz's work, we were introduced to IDEC and to the many U.S., European, Middle Eastern and Asian offshoots of IDEC.

Holt Associates, Inc. was the brainchild of John Holt who started it in 1971. "I have never let my schooling interfere with my education," Mark Twain is alleged to have said, and I am sure that John Holt would have agreed. In 1977, after having taught in schools and written numerous books on the subject, John started publishing a networking newsletter, "Growing Without Schooling "(GWS). It was then that he cast the world of school aside in favor of home schooling, more specifically, unschooling. His book, *Teach Your Own*, is known and read all over the world.

GWS was closer to the size of a magazine than a newsletter. It became a prime source of information about how children learn, how children fail, and what parents might do to change things for themselves and for their families. Those who strove to incorporate living with learning were particularly drawn to and well-served by Holt Associates. They shared with one another, through stories and reports in GWS, how school practices (textbooks, class routines, tests, and the like) could be abandoned in favor of child-directed activities and the natural flow of daily home life

In 1980, Holt Associates added John Holt's Book and Music Store which offered unusual books and materials for and about children.

Pat Farenga worked closely with John as a member of the Holt Associates staff, and when John died in 1985, Pat assumed the position of President. He reorganized Holt Associates, Inc. as HoltGWS LLC. Pat and his wife, Day, homeschooled their three children. Pat is himself a writer as well as a consultant and an advocate for homeschooling. He has overseen the metamorphosis of Holt Associates in its evolution to today, continuing service to educators and homeschoolers the world over.

Clonlara is indebted to Holt Associates from its inauguration by John Holt to its latter-day involvement in Clonlara's life by Pat Farenga. Pat served our staff as a consultant for some months at the turn of the Century and he has remained a close friend. Our staff was enriched, too, with the arrival of Susannah Sheffer who had been a volunteer at Holt Associates before accepting a position with Clonlara in the Nineties.

The listings above are not all-inclusive by any means. There were numerous state and national individuals and groups whose work supported both or either of the two movements—free school and homeschool —over the years. Those on this list were the main ones that were nearest and dearest to Clonlara and to me. They each in their own way foster and promote the time-honored philosophies of the giants upon whose shoulders we stand.

9

THE BEAT GOES ON

Following the sudden death of my sister, Kitty, in 1991, I spent the next several years just going through the motions. The exceptional staff, led mainly by Billie Fahrner in the CSHBEP office, and Nat Needle in the campus school, carried on during my daze (which lasted for about five years, give or take a few).

When the fog of mourning lifted I became ever more aware of the toll that time had taken on the four buildings at the end of Jewett Street. Both of the frame dwellings had had to be retro-fitted for our purposes in the first place, and they were added to willy-nilly from time to time. The two "tin can" units (aka portable classrooms) had been purchased from the Ann Arbor Public Schools and from Washtenaw Community College, respectively. Each had been well used before we got them. The place had a shaggy air about it—as though kids were in charge (I glibly said).

By this time, the CSHBEP was pulling its own weight, financially speaking, and its income was enough to partially fund the campus school operations. I made a trip to the bank downtown where Clonlara had its accounts, spoke to a loan officer, and put the question before him: Can the National Bank finance a sorely-needed new building? He pored over the figures for a while and then told me there was no way that he could take that risk. Schools cannot count on their clientele in the same way that churches cannot count on continued enrollment. No loan possible!

Piqued, I stepped out onto the sidewalk and surveyed my surroundings. Clonlara had invested in this bank, thought I; but this bank will not invest in Clonlara. Huh! Directly across the street stood Comerica Bank. I walked over, asked to see the bank president, James Miller, and told him that I was interested in moving Clonlara's account to Comerica Bank. Oh, and would he consider financing a new building? Mr. Miller listened politely. He inquired about the operations on Jewett Street, commented on the length of time that the programs had existed and about why we did what we did. He promised to examine the account as soon as the transfer was complete, and he'd get back to me.

It wasn't long afterwards that the children led a visitor in a dark blue suit, white shirt and tie to my office in the blue house. He had been walking the property and chatting with the staff and students he met. It was Jim Miller, President of Comerica Bank, paying a call.

He told me that he had considered the loan request, had come to see for himself, and had made up his mind during his visit. Yes, Comerica would fund a new building to the tune of 1.2 million dollars.

Things moved rather quickly then. Billie and I interviewed, among others, the architectural firm of Hobbs and

Black and the construction firm of O'Neal, and chose them both for the job. We—designers, builders, Clonlara staff members and administrators from both programs—met to advise, counsel, assess, price, review blueprints, etc.— regularly. Students and parents from both programs were welcomed to join; each group was, thereby, represented.

My instruction to the designer was: make this building as unlike a school as you can. We learned that a building in Finland that served as a school had received architectural awards, so I asked Bill from Hobbs and Black to take a trip there to see it. He did. The results can be seen in the number of windows which bring the light of day into view no matter where one stands, in the "garden atrium" that comprises the middle-most room, and in the skylights throughout.

In 1997, the ribbon cutting in front of the new building took place. It housed both the campus school and the home based program under one roof, and it was spanking new. Staff, parents and students marveled at how file carts with wheels would now stay right where they were placed without moving down slanted floors anymore. The furnishings were still ragtag, but the edifice was superb.

Just a few years ago, I met up with Jim Miller at a senior center event on the north campus of the University of Michigan. I asked him how it was that he decided those years back to lend Clonlara the money when another bank would not. He said,

> I knew from your description that this was a place that didn't play by the same rules as ordinary businesses. I also knew your request posed a risk for the bank.

> When I came to observe, I could feel the spirit of love and caring alive in the place, and I told myself it was time for me to step outside of the box.

By this time, Jim Montgomery had worked for almost 40 years as a Foreign Student Adviser at the University of Michigan's International Center. He was taking steps to retire from his post, and he was spending more and more time with our two grandsons. The time was right for me to do likewise.

I had learned from Sandy Hurst, founder of Upattinas School in Glenmoore, Pennsylvania a lot about transitions. She introduced me to the works of William Bridges, Peter Senge, and Margaret Wheatley.[1] Following Sandy's lead, I introduced these authors' books to staff members and, together, we set the stage for my transitioning out of the everyday work of Clonlara.

First, we looked around at what Clonlara had become and what work that it was then doing. From a nursery school with eight children enrolled (1967), it had grown into a multi-service agency. Most campus staff and students were not fully aware of the work that the home based program staff was doing in the offices at the other end of

---

[1] *Leadership and the New Science*, by Margaret J. Wheatley, Berrett-Koelher Publishers, San Francisco, CA, 1999

The Fifth Discipline, by Peter M. Senge, Currency/Doubleday Publishers, New York, NY, 1990

Transitions, by William Bridges, Da Capo Press, Cambridge, MA, 2004

the building. Peter Senge's warning spoke to us: "When people in organizations focus only on their position, they have little sense of responsibility for the results produced when all positions interact."

We charted each of the programs: the parents, students, and staff in each, and the specific tasks they worked to accomplish as well as where this work was done. There were:

> Clonlara campus parents, students and teachers in Ann Arbor
>
> Clonlara School Home Based Education parents and students in 45 States and in 32 countries
>
> Clonlara teacher/advisers in Michigan, West Virginia, Indiana, Illinois, Colorado, Germany, France, Spain and Japan
>
> Clonlara campus administrators
>
> Clonlara home based administrators
>
> Clonlara Governing Board members
>
> Clonlara Advisory Team
>
> Clonlara Building and Grounds Team

A representative from each of these groups was chosen by the group itself (or volunteered for the post and was accepted by the group). Each was asked to commit to attending two meetings a month for however long the process took. Each meeting was to be 1½ hours long.

This group, called The Transition Team, consisted of ten members (sometimes eleven when a second campus student felt the urge). Next, we laid out the general framework:

1) Compile a thorough report of the nature and scope of each group's daily work at/for Clonlara,

2) Cite areas of success and areas that need attention and/or change,

3) Prepare that information; present it at the designated meeting,

4) Examine, discuss, and offer suggestions/solutions,

5) Read the suggested books and materials available to all,

6) Report back to respective groups and seek input from members.

7) Lay concrete plans for Clonlara's future.

Our purpose was to share with one another those parts of our relatively sprawling establishment to determine how each contributed to making Clonlara the vital, living service it was meant to be. We learned from our readings that organizations, like the humans who run them, are living entities. They undergo changes over time and if they are led through major changes with care, they will survive and grow and develop holistically.

When an organization has been run mainly by the person who founded it, the change in leadership could prove to be life-threatening if it did not involve the others who held positions of leadership in it. The people that it served, we learned, should also be part of the dialogue of change.

Each author virtually guaranteed that the next stage of such an organization would look significantly different from the earlier one. Its perspective would shift from that of a visionary to more of an administrative one. Most founders lack, for example, a secure sense of business. If I hadn't ever realized that along the way, I certainly learned it during this process. The writing was clearly on the wall!

A professor of organizational behavior at the University of Michigan, Dearborn, Dr. Jerry Lapides, agreed to work with the transition team for three months. He helped us apply the principles of Senge and Wheatley to Clonlara during this time of change. He held several seminars with the transition team. He pored through the activities we were engaged in, and he made suggestions for others as well.

One and a half years into the process—in May 2005—the team reached the point of determining what Clonlara's future would look like, and it laid out the map for what the governance would look like and what qualifications would be required of whomever stepped into its leadership role. The first decision was that there would have to be a leader for the campus program and a leader for the home based program.

My daughter, Chandra Montgomery Nicol, served on the transition team as the representative of Clonlara's Board of Trustees. She took her turn as scribe for the May meeting, and duly listed on the whiteboard the responses to the question: what are we looking for in a leader who will head up the home based office? Looking at the list, Terri Wheeler, representative of home based administration, said, "Chandra, you might as well just put your name up there as the answer to that search because you have all of those qualifications. There is no one else who does or could." The choice was finalized at the next, and last, meeting when all present agreed. The path forward was clear.

A mere three days had passed when a woman who had served as Director at Community High, the Ann Arbor Public School's alternative high school, walked into the building asking whether or not there might be a position for her at Clonlara. She had not even heard that we were about to begin a search, she said. Divine Providence at work yet again! She was interviewed by transition team members and hired for the second position, Director of the campus school.

Terry Wheeler and I sat in my office one day, reminiscing about years gone by and the new chapter that was poised to begin. "What is one of the treasures that you are most proud of as you prepare to leave?" she asked. That took some mulling.

I finally glommed onto a nugget that often ran across my mind when I was blessed to be working still with the campus students. It is a trailer to that event which took place in 1967 at the University of Michigan School of Education. The professor asked why I was starting a school and what would be different about that school. When I told her that my aim was to help youngsters develop into happy people, she rolled her eyes and asked how one quantifies happiness. "It is not measurable, and can't be scientifically studied," she said. Happiness was, in her analysis, an ambiguous, touchy-feely, elusive somethin-gorother that can be interpreted in as many ways as a person chooses. "I will know it when I see it," had been my response at the time.

Little did I know then of the work of neuroscientists who were researching the measurable effects of inner well-being on body and mind. Scientists like Matthieu Ricard, a molecular biologist. His research combined science with spirit—modern psychological research coupled with Buddhist thought. In his book, *Happiness, a Guide to Developing Life's Most Important Skill*,[2] he makes a passionate case for happiness as a goal.

> By happiness I mean a deep sense of flourishing that arises from an exceptionally healthy mind. This is not a mere pleasurable feeling, a fleeting emotion or a mood, but an optimal state of being. Happiness is also a way of interpreting the world, since while it may be difficult to change the world, it is always possible to change the way we look at it. (p.19)

Ricard exposes the false and limited notions we have about our potential as human beings. The goal of life, he says, "is a deep state of well-being and wisdom," accompanied by "love for every human being." It arises from an essential goodness "that wholeheartedly desires everyone to find meaning in their lives." Striving to find happiness is a skill that deserves at least as much energy as any other we seek to hone. Amen, I say. This was precisely what I meant by "I'll know it when I see it."

---

2 Matthieu Ricard, *Happiness, A Guide to Developing Life's Most Important Skill*, 2003

Yet another of the facts of my life at Clonlara that surfaced during my "exit" days was a more mundane, less philosophical one in nature. Throughout the years, and regardless of where I set up an office desk—sometimes a corner of a room, and occasionally in a room of its own—the area around and atop the desk was notoriously messy. Horizontal filing, people named it. Somewhere on the side of my outsized desk, a staff member had taped a poster which read, "If a cluttered desk is a sign of a cluttered mind, what is an empty desk the sign of?" My perfect excuse!!

In the Nineties, I inherited Kitty's upstairs office in one of the frame buildings. Jim fielded a telephone call in the wee hours of the morning, at our home. The fire alarm had gone off at the school and the police were on their way. Could we come out to unlock the doors? We bundled up and met them on Jewett Street. They entered the house and searched every area. Nothing. No break-in. Everything seemed to be in order. The second officer just had to finish checking the upstairs room and we could lock up and leave. It must have been a racoon or a squirrel that set off the alarm.

Then the officer called from upstairs. Yes, he said, this room is completely trashed. He summoned us to view the damages. I had to explain to the three men that what they were witnessing was not the result of a break-in. It was the usual condition of my office. We all left in silence. That true tale sets the scene for a the call I received many years later. The librarian from the Bentley Historical Library at the University of Michigan was on the line. This time, I was speaking from my relatively swank office in the new building.

"Would you consider donating your papers to the Bentley Library?" the caller asked. I cast my eyes across the two-inch deep, randomly tossed stacks of paper, then down to the several, overflowing boxes hugging the walls beneath the windows, past the rows of books that didn't fit on the shelves above, and back. I was chuckling aloud when I described the scene to the librarian. I asked whether he'd want to wade through all of that. Yes, he would, and he would search through files and boxes, through storage spaces to locate audio tapes, video tapes, brochures, binders, policy manuals, court cases, through attic nooks and cubby holes... everywhere, everything. His team would sort through what they found worth taking and dispose of the rest (if that was what I wanted). Imagine my delight.

The Bentley Library cleared the lion's share of my clutter and carted it away to their collection across town. Their librarians catalogued all of Clonlara's paraphernalia in the library's historical collection—a miniscule part of the vast array of materials it has amassed over the decades—since 1935. Students and scholars seeking to understand the history of the State of Michigan can access these materials. It is comforting to know that these things were salvaged, almost certainly, from the recycling bin, and that they just may be of interest to someone, sometime.

In July of 2006, thirty-nine plus years after I had started, I cleared the last carton from my office and ceded it to Chandra. I exited the building that day thinking that I ought to be shedding a tear or feeling some sort of tug at my heartstrings, but I felt only the front door swishing shut behind me. I remembered, too, a hand-printed sign on a

Xerox banner that a staff member had made and hung in one of the old portable classrooms where the staff usually met in those days. It read: "If you must leave, leave quietly. The rest of us are staying here." *That* was a very comforting thought for me then, indeed.

Now they can create the school that is inside them just as I had the pleasure of doing. Clonlara celebrates its 50th anniversary this year, 2017. I count my blessings!

STATEMENTS FROM PAST STUDENTS AND PARENTS

Both of my children, now successful adults, are graduates of Clonlara's distance learning program. My son works for our family owned radio stations and has a professional photography business of his own. He is married with three children. My daughter started a very successful performing arts center where she teaches dance, theater, singing, and piano. She encourages her students to find their way not only in the arts but also in life. Without Clonlara's philosophy on growth, learning, and expression, I am not sure that they would be the successful entrepreneurs that they are. Clonlara gives students the confidence they need to be successful in all their life long endeavors.

—*Shirley M.*,
parent, home school graduates, New York

My boy attended Clonlara campus school for four years. He transferred there as a 9th grader. At the time, he was experiencing a lack of motivation due to the death of his father. He came into the school with a bit of an attitude. He was not motivated to apply himself. I did not understand the concept of Clonlara when I enrolled him, but after trusting my son and trusting Clonlara, I am happy to say that he graduated having achieved more than I could have dreamed possible. It took more than the first year for me to truly understand how it works. Seeing the results of a balanced, motivated, confident young man who is working and ready to attend college, is close to miraculous.

—Kelli C.,
parent, campus school graduate, Michigan

A lot of people feel like [school] wastes their time or that classes aren't relevant, so they lose interest and start focusing on things that don't actually matter to them. Whereas, when you graduate from Clonlara, you don't feel like, "Finally, I'm done, I'm free," because you were already free. You feel like, "Wow, I used and implemented this tool to the best of my abilities, and I had a really good time doing it."

—*Everett D.,*
campus school graduate, Michigan

In Clonlara, I was able to study whatever I wanted, however I wanted. It was unique and special, because I could manage my time and follow my interests. I loved being my own boss. I'm starting my sophomore year this fall at The University of Southern Mississippi (Criminal Justice major). Thanks to Clonlara, I could prepare for my TOEFL and SAT exams, along with all the other college application processes. I also got used to working/studying independently.

—*Viktoria P.,*
distance learning graduate, Hungary

I enjoyed my time at Clonlara. I was a competitive gymnast, so I trained nearly every day. Clonlara allowed me time to train and learn without worry. Because of Clonlara, I was able to become one of the top ten gymnasts in my region and get into a good university where I am working in research and development for Nestle International. I have been able to travel to Europe and across the United States for this job. Through Clonlara, I learned to follow my passion.

—*Ryan S.,*
distance learning graduate, Ohio

Clonlara was remarkable in several ways, the first being its commitment to the fundamental principle that children and people enjoy learning, and that the efficacy of educational experiences is maximized when these are facilitated, as opposed to mandated. I am currently a Firefighter/Paramedic and Adjunct Emergency Medical Services Faculty for a community college. Emergency services are notorious for the requirement to become quickly and completely competent in a multitude of diverse disciplines, which include fire science, emergency medicine, hazardous materials management, wildland firefighting, and technical rescue. Each of these disciplines has required curriculum and certifying tests, as well as continuing education requirements. The spirit of lifelong learning that I acquired from Clonlara has served me tremendously in this profession.

—*Landon C*,
distance learning graduate, Colorado

At Clonlara I had the complete freedom to design my own education and to explore a wide variety of interests with the supportive counsel of my teacher-advisor. Because I "owned" my education, I developed a passion for learning that wouldn't have been possible in a traditional environment. I attended law school and am currently employed in the legal profession. Clonlara taught me to make my own educational decisions and to direct my learning. It made me fearless about venturing into new educational territory.
—*Roberto V.,*
distance learning graduate, Arizona

I am the pastor for a new church in Olympia, WA. My time with Clonlara allowed me to be self-motivated and driven to achieve my goals.

—Elizabeth S.,
home school graduate, Washington

I now own a small IT Company. Clonlara helped me develop the self discipline to accomplish that.

—Michael H,
distance learning graduate, Germany

I love the flexibility of being able to use real world experiences as part of my education. I graduated from Wayne State University with my Master's in Psychology. I'm now a school psychologist, helping other school staff better understand the needs of students. I took a Clonlara campus class, "Herstory." It was an awesome, experiential way to learn about the past.

— *Emily R,* graduate, combined program: campus/home school, Michigan

Clonlara was a perfect fit for me, due to its flexibility. Not only was I able to explore the topics in which I had a genuine interest (I studied anatomy and physiology in grade 9 and genetics in grade 10), but I also got to incorporate my passions for music and theatre into my education - passions which would have been mere extracurricular activities in another program. The ability to design my own courses and supplement book learning with "real world" experiences made my high school years a fulfilling time. The flexibility of Clonlara showed me that one always has more options than one thinks. When I was working on my graduation portfolio, I sorted through four years' worth of drawings, photographs, writing, and tickets from concerts, plays, and museums. Looking back on everything I had learned and accomplished felt amazing.

—*Siyuan C-P.*,
distance learning graduate, Canada